CLASSROOM DATA TRACKING

Data-Tracking Tools at Your Fingertips!

Grade 2

Carson-Dellosa Publishing, LLC
PO Box 35665
Greensboro, NC 27425 USA
carsondellosa.com

978-1-4838-3440-5
01-158161151

Table of Contents

© Carson-Dellosa • CD-104918

What Is Classroom Data Tracking?

Being able to prove student growth is more important than ever, making classroom data tracking essential in today's classroom. Data tracking is capturing student learning through both formative and summative assessments and displaying the results. Further assessment of the results can then become an active part of teaching, planning, and remediation. Because teachers are accountable to families and administrators, and time is always at a premium in the classroom, using a simple yet comprehensive data-tracking system is a must.

This book will help make this important data-collection task manageable. The data-tracking tools—charts, rubrics, logs, checklists, inventories, etc.—are easy to use and modifiable to fit any classroom. The tools will help you collect quantitative and qualitative information on each student's level of mastery in any part of your curriculum. Having specific details at your fingertips will aid in setting goals with students, keeping families informed, updating administrators, and displaying progress at student conferences.

An important component of good classroom data tracking is involving students in their own progress so that they can take ownership of their learning. Statistics prove that when students monitor their own learning and track their own growth, they are more highly motivated and perform better. In addition, a good data-tracking system presents avenues for celebrating student successes. Such opportunities are presented here, whether with an "I've done it!" check box or a rating score, and serve to create the intrinsic motivation we all want to see in students.

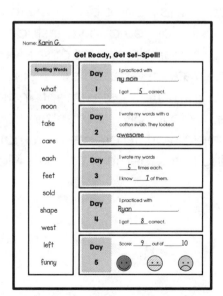

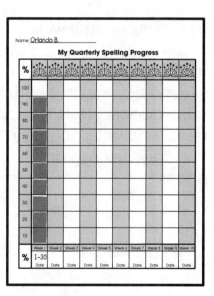

Completed data-tracking sheets for spelling

Why Should I Use Data Tracking?

Teachers are busy and do not need new tasks, but data tracking is a must because in today's data-driven classroom, information is crucial. Fortunately, classroom data tracking can be an at-your-disposal, invaluable tool in many ways:

- Data tracking creates a growth mindset. It shifts focus from a pass/fail mentality to one of showing growth over time.
- It allows you to see any gaps in concepts that need reteaching so that you can easily create focused remediation groups.
- It allows for more targeted lesson planning for the upcoming weeks. Pre-assessments can help you justify spending little to no time on skills that students have already mastered or more time on skills where students lack the expected baseline knowledge. Post-assessments can also help you determine whether students need more time or, if not, what topics you should address next.
- It provides you with daily information and allows you to give students feedback and guidance more regularly.
- It involves students with tracking their own data so that they can easily see their own progress.
- It gives students a sense of pride and ownership over their learning.
- It helps create data portfolios that are useful tools for families, administrators, and student conferences.

Data Tracking in Your Classroom

As standards become more rigorous, data tracking is becoming a necessary part of an already full daily classroom routine. The pages in this book are intended as tools that will help you manage your classroom data and create a customized system to make data tracking more manageable. This book is designed to allow you to choose the reproducibles that work specifically for you and your students. You may even choose to use some reproducibles only for certain groups of students instead of the entire class. This book also allows you to integrate assessments into your current routines by using informal observations and other formative assessments instead of interrupting the flow with traditional tests. If possible, try to involve students in tracking their own data by using reproducibles, graphs, and sample work to create and manage their own portfolios (for more detailed data-tracking management tips, see Managing Data Tracking on pages 8–9).

How to Use This Book

This book includes four main types of pages. Refer to the following sample pages and descriptions to help you get the most out of this resource.

Each anchor and domain section begins with a learning crosswalk. Use the crosswalk to help you better understand what students should know from the previous year and what they will need to know for the next year to better guide your plans for teaching, assessment, and remediation.

- -

A concepts checklist follows the crosswalk for each anchor and domain. Use the checklist to track which concepts you have taught and when. Write the standard code (such as OA.A.1) in the top-left box and describe the concept in the large space. Use some or all of the boxes to the right to list the dates that you taught, tested, and retaught the concept. Make multiple copies as needed.

- -

An explanation page precedes each set of three reproducibles. Use this page to learn about the intended use for each reproducible, to find additional suggestions for use, and to see an example of each reproducible in use.

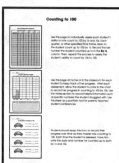

- -

The type of reproducibles included for each concept will vary according to the types of reproducibles that are most useful for assessing that concept. Reproducibles may include whole-class recording sheets, conference sheets, open-ended assessment pages, or pages where students take charge of their own goals and learning. Use the explanation page before each set to better understand how to use each page.

- -

In addition, use the Standards Assessed chart on page 10 to plan for and keep track of the standards and related assessments for a single subject at a glance. Simply record all of the standards for the subject, the dates taught, and any other brief notes you choose to record (assessment types, overall class proficiency, etc.).

Getting Started

You can start data tracking at any point in the school year. If you are new to data tracking, it may be helpful to start small with a single subject until you become more comfortable with the process. Use the following guidelines to help you start a data-tracking system in your classroom (for more detailed data-tracking management tips, see Managing Data Tracking on pages 8–9).

1. Choose the best format for your classroom.

You may choose to have a single binder to collect data or have individual student binders or folders (for more information, see Which Format Is Best? on page 7).

2. Add a cover page.

Because the data-tracking binder will play a starring role in your school year, design an attractive cover that will make the binder identifiable and enjoyable to use. If students are also creating binders or folders, have them add cover pages as well.

3. Organize the binder(s) into sections.

Decide what subjects and topics you will be assessing and use tabs or dividers to clearly divide and label them.

4. Choose a rating system.

Although you may use different systems depending on what and how you will be assessing, use a single rating system for the majority of assessments to create consistency, cohesiveness, and clarity.

Use the following guidelines to help you set a clear tone for the year if using student binders as well.

5. Compose guidelines or a "mission statement."

Guidelines or a short "mission statement" will let students know what is expected of them and make them accountable with their data tracking. If desired, have students keep copies at the beginning of their notebooks and have both students and family members sign them at the beginning of the school year.

6. Have students set long-term and short-term goals.

Long-term goals will give students targets to work toward. Short-term goals will give students attainable checkpoints along the way. It may also be helpful to give students standards checklists in student-friendly language and to have students keep written goals in their binders as reminders.

Other Suggestions

Here are some additional important elements to consider before beginning a data-tracking system:

- *How to recognize students for their successes throughout the year.* Consider ideas such as placing stars programmed with students' names on a Reaching for the Stars bulletin board, giving special rewards, or giving verbal recognition along with a unique class cheer.

- *How to include families in this endeavor.* It can be as simple as sending letters home at the beginning of the year, having student-led conferences using the data binders, or sharing goals with families so that students can work on their goals at home as well.

- *How to maintain student binders.* It may be helpful to provide students with rubrics at the beginning of the year, outlining the expectations for maintaining and assessing their binders periodically to make sure that they continue to include samples and keep the binders neat and organized.

- *How to store student binders.* Decide where to keep the binders—at students' desks or in a separate location. If keeping them in a separate location, you may need to set guidelines for when students can access and add to them.

Which Format Is Best?

Because classroom data-tracking systems need to last for an entire year, many teachers create and maintain them in three-ring binders because of their durability. However, you may choose to keep student work in folders if space is an issue or if students will be storing less information.

A Single Teacher Binder	A Teacher Binder and Student Binders
Pros • Convenient format means the information can always be with you. • You can store all of the information in one place.	**Pros** • Students can move sample work with them each year. • You can include more information because space is not limited. • You have less to do when preparing for conferences.
Cons • You have to gather student work when preparing for conferences. • Space is limited.	**Cons** • It can be time-consuming to work with numerous binders. • It can be challenging to assess class proficiency when sample work is in individual binders.

Managing Data Tracking

Managing the Teacher Binder

- Choose a durable two- or three-inch binder to store all of the important information for the whole year.

- Use the teacher binder as the one place to store the following important assessment-related tools and reproducibles:
  - a copy of the standards at the front of your binder for easy reference
  - copies of the resources and assessment tools for your grade, such as pacing guides, word lists, fluency tests, and reading level charts
  - master copies of assessments (You may also choose to store these separately for space reasons.)

- Consider separating the binder into two sections—overall class proficiency and individual student data. In the class proficiency section, keep information such as what standards you taught and when, overall class scores, and student grouping information. Use the individual student section to store running records, baseline tests, remediation forms, and anecdotal notes.

- At the beginning of the school year, assign students numbers and use a set of numbered tabs to organize individual student data in a single place. Add a copy of student names and assigned numbers to the front of the individual data section.

Managing Student Binders

- Consider copying yearlong tracking sheets on card stock instead of copy paper for durability.

- Color code sections to make it easier for students to quickly find the correct pages. For example, copy all sight word pages on yellow paper.

- For younger students, have volunteers preassemble the binders. Include all of the tracking sheets for the year (even if you won't use some until later) to avoid having to add pages later.

- Provide students with several three-hole-punched page protectors for storing sample work, which is often not prepunched.

- Devote a short, designated time each week to allow students to add sample work to and organize their binders.

Tips and Tricks

Organize everything.
- Use file folders to create dividing tabs in a binder. Cut off the half of a file folder with the tab, three-hole punch it, and place it in your binder.
- Keep binders simple by using one pocket for each subject.

Save time.
- Use pens in different colors to make recording dates on a recording sheet simpler. Instead of writing the same date numerous times, simply write the date once in one color and record all of the data from that day using that color. If adding data from another date, repeat with a different color.
- Choose a standard proficiency scale and use it consistently throughout the binder. For example:

E, P, M (emerging, progressing, mastered)	NS, B, OL, A (not seen, beginning, on level, above)
✓-, ✓, ✓+	−, +, ++
a 0–4 rubric	your own unique system

Fit assessment into your day.
- Keep sheets of large labels (such as 2" x 4") on a clipboard. Carry the clipboard throughout the day and use the labels to record any informal observations about individual students. Record each student's name, the date, and your observation on a label. At the end of the day, simply place the label in the corresponding student's section.
- Use your weekly or monthly plan to copy the relevant whole-class progress charts and conference sheets ahead of time. Keep them on a clipboard so that they are at hand when observing students throughout the week or month.
- Focus on assessing or observing only three to five students per day.

Make the reproducibles work for your classroom.
- Add text before copying to create a unique assessment.
- Add, remove, or alter items such as write-on lines or date lines.
- Use a different scale than suggested (see the table above for ideas).
- Use pencil when recording on whole-class checklists so that it is simple to change marks as students progress.
- Use highlighters to draw attention to skills that need remediation, to an individual student's areas of need, or to create targeted small groups.
- Highlight or add stickers beside student goals on graphs and other tracking sheets to give students something visible to work toward.

Standards Assessed

Subject_____ **Quarter**_____

Standard/Topic	Date	Date	Date	Date	Notes

Name: _____   Date: _____

Second Grade Math
Skills Inventory

Skip Counting   ☐ 5s   ☐ 10s   ☐ 100s

☐ +   ☐ −   by 10 or 100 mentally

Addition
☐ up to tens   ☐ with regrouping
☐ up to hundreds   ☐ with regrouping
☐ up to four two-digit addends

Subtraction
☐ up to tens   ☐ with regrouping
☐ up to hundreds   ☐ with regrouping

Measurement
☐ can choose appropriate tools
☐ can estimate lengths
☐ can measure length

Tells time to the nearest
☐ hour   ☐ half hour   ☐ five minutes
☐ can use *am* and *pm*

Identify
25¢   1¢   5¢   10¢ $1 $5
☐ can count money

Can Create
☐ line plot   ☐ bar graph   ☐ picture graph
☐ can interpret data on a graph

☐ Understands odd and even

Arrays
☐ can find total
☐ can write related equation

☐ +   ☐ −   within 20 fluently

Understands
☐ ones   ☐ tens   ☐ hundreds

Can read and write
☐ numerals
☐ word form
☐ expanded form

Can compare numbers to
☐ tens   ☐ hundreds

Identify

☐ can partition shapes equally
☐ can name partitions

Name: _____

Second Grade Language Arts
Skills Inventory

Reading Level _____

Fluency _____

Comprehension
- ☐ understands key details
- ☐ knows story elements
- ☐ understands story structure (beginning, middle, end)
- ☐ recounts stories
- ☐ tells main idea
- ☐ finds central message
- ☐ compares and contrasts
- ☐ identifies author's purpose

Simple Sentences	Compound Sentences
☐ produce	☐ produce
☐ expand	☐ expand
☐ rearrange	☐ rearrange

When writing, correctly uses
- ☐ capitalization
- ☐ ending punctuation
- ☐ commas

Foundations
- ☐ distinguishes long and short vowel sounds
- ☐ identifies syllables in a word
- ☐ knows vowel teams

ai	au	aw	ay	ea
ee	ei	eu	ew	ey
ie	oa	oe	oo	ou
ow	oy	ue	ui	VCe

Can identify and use
- ☐ nouns
- ☐ collective nouns
- ☐ irregular plural nouns

- ☐ pronouns
- ☐ reflexive pronouns

- ☐ verbs
- ☐ irregular verbs

- ☐ adjectives
- ☐ adverbs

Can form and use
- ☐ compound words
- ☐ contractions
- ☐ possessives

Operations and Algebraic Thinking
Standards Crosswalk

First Grade

Represent and solve problems involving addition and subtraction.
- Use addition and subtraction within 20 to solve word problems with unknowns in all positions (including those represented by a symbol).
- Solve addition word problems with three numbers whose sum is less than or equal to 20.

Understand and apply properties of operations and the relationship between addition and subtraction.
- Apply properties of operations as strategies to add and subtract.
- Understand subtraction as an unknown-addend problem.

Add and subtract within 20.
- Relate counting to addition and subtraction.
- Use strategies to add and subtract within 20.
- Demonstrate fluency with addition and subtraction within 10.

Work with addition and subtraction equations.
- Understand the meaning of the equal sign.
- Determine if addition and subtraction equations are true or false.
- Find the unknown number in addition and subtraction equations.

Third Grade

Represent and solve problems involving multiplication and division.
- Interpret products of whole numbers.
- Interpret whole-number quotients of whole numbers.
- Use multiplication and division within 100 to solve word problems.
- Determine the unknown whole number in a multiplication or division equation relating three whole numbers.

Understand properties of multiplication and the relationship between multiplication and division.
- Apply properties of operations as strategies to multiply and divide.
- Understand division as an unknown-factor problem.

Multiply and divide within 100.
- Fluently multiply and divide within 100.
- Memorize all products of two one-digit numbers.

Solve problems involving the four operations and identify and explain patterns in arithmetic.
- Use the four operations to solve two-step word problems with a variable used to represent the unknown quantity.
- Use strategies to decide if an answer is reasonable.
- Identify arithmetic patterns and explain them using properties of operations.

Operations and Algebraic Thinking
Concepts Checklist

Concept		Date(s) Taught				

Word Problems

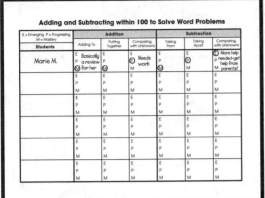

This sheet is ideal for keeping an eye on the strategies that students need for solving word problems. Record each student's name in the left-hand column. After rating a student's progress, use the remainder of the space for comments.

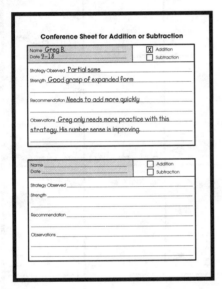

Attach copies of this conference sheet to a clipboard for easy note-taking on spot observations you make during classroom work. Record the date and student's name and check off which operation you are observing. Be sure to note strengths, areas to focus on, and specific observations.

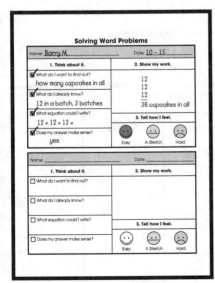

Have students complete this form after they complete word problems you have given them. Clip the word problems to this sheet or print them on an adhesive label and attach them to the back. This will help you make sense of the notes later.

Adding and Subtracting within 100 to Solve Word Problems

E = Emerging P = Progressing
M = Mastery

Students	Addition							Subtraction					
	Adding To			Putting Together			Comparing, with Unknowns			Taking From			Taking Apart			Comparing, with Unknowns
	E P M	E P M	E P M	E P M	E P M	E P M
	E P M	E P M	E P M	E P M	E P M	E P M
	E P M	E P M	E P M	E P M	E P M	E P M
	E P M	E P M	E P M	E P M	E P M	E P M
	E P M	E P M	E P M	E P M	E P M	E P M
	E P M	E P M	E P M	E P M	E P M	E P M

16

© Carson-Dellosa • CD-104918

Conference Sheet for Addition or Subtraction

Name _____

Date _____

☐ Addition

☐ Subtraction

Strategy Observed _____

Strength _____

_____

Recommendation _____

_____

Observations _____

_____

_____

Name _____

Date _____

☐ Addition

☐ Subtraction

Strategy Observed _____

Strength _____

_____

Recommendation _____

_____

Observations _____

_____

_____

Solving Word Problems

Name: _____ Date: _____

1. Think about it.	2. Show my work.
☐ What do I want to find out?	
☐ What do I already know?	
☐ What equation could I write?	**3. Tell how I feel.**
☐ Does my answer make sense?	Easy A Stretch Hard

Name: _____ Date: _____

1. Think about it.	2. Show my work.
☐ What do I want to find out?	
☐ What do I already know?	
☐ What equation could I write?	**3. Tell how I feel.**
☐ Does my answer make sense?	Easy A Stretch Hard

   © Carson-Dellosa • CD-104918

Working with Equal Groups of Objects

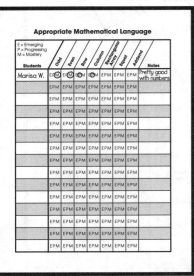

Appropriate academic vocabulary is necessary to help students understand the mathematical concepts you are introducing. Record student names in the left-hand column. When beginning a unit, introduce the essential new vocabulary and then allow students time to work with the concepts. This form will allow you to see at a glance which students have mastered the vocabulary and which need extra help.

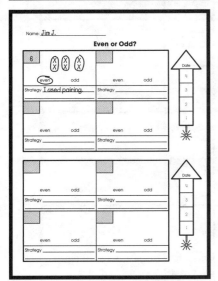

Various strategies can help students figure out whether a number is odd or even. After you have introduced several strategies to students, have them complete this sheet to show what they know. Write a number in the top left-hand box. Students should first use any strategy to assess the number and then circle *odd* or *even*. Students should briefly write which strategy they used in their own words. You may also use this sheet as a pretest and posttest if desired.

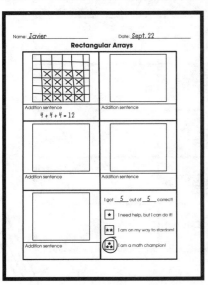

Use this form to teach or assess rectangular arrays. Draw a grid of any size in each rectangle. Use an X (or other mark) to fill in an array on the grid. Ask students to make an addition sentence to express the total as a sum of equal addends. Finally, have students assess themselves by stating how many they got right of the number given and by coloring or circling a star box.

Appropriate Mathematical Language

E = Emerging
P = Progressing
M = Mastery

Students	Odd	Even	Row	Column	Rectangular Array	Equal	Addend	Notes
	EPM	EPM	EPM	EPM	EPM	EPM	EPM	
	EPM	EPM	EPM	EPM	EPM	EPM	EPM	
	EPM	EPM	EPM	EPM	EPM	EPM	EPM	
	EPM	EPM	EPM	EPM	EPM	EPM	EPM	
	EPM	EPM	EPM	EPM	EPM	EPM	EPM	
	EPM	EPM	EPM	EPM	EPM	EPM	EPM	
	EPM	EPM	EPM	EPM	EPM	EPM	EPM	
	EPM	EPM	EPM	EPM	EPM	EPM	EPM	
	EPM	EPM	EPM	EPM	EPM	EPM	EPM	
	EPM	EPM	EPM	EPM	EPM	EPM	EPM	
	EPM	EPM	EPM	EPM	EPM	EPM	EPM	
	EPM	EPM	EPM	EPM	EPM	EPM	EPM	
	EPM	EPM	EPM	EPM	EPM	EPM	EPM	
	EPM	EPM	EPM	EPM	EPM	EPM	EPM	
	EPM	EPM	EPM	EPM	EPM	EPM	EPM	

Name: _____

Even or Odd?

even odd	even odd
Strategy _____	Strategy _____
even odd	even odd
Strategy _____	Strategy _____

Date
4
3
2
1

even odd	even odd
Strategy _____	Strategy _____
even odd	even odd
Strategy _____	Strategy _____

Date
4
3
2
1

Rectangular Arrays

Addition sentence

Addition sentence

Addition sentence

Addition sentence

Addition sentence

I got _____ out of _____ correct!

★ I need help, but I can do it!

★★ I am on my way to stardom!

★★★ I am a math champion!

Number and Operations in Base Ten
Standards Crosswalk

First Grade

Extend the counting sequence.
- Read, write, count, and represent numbers from 0 to 120.

Understand place value.
- Understand that the digits of a two-digit number represent tens and ones.
- Understand that the numbers 11 to 19 are made of a 10 and a set of ones.
- Relate counting by 10s to place value.
- Compare two two-digit numbers using >, <, and =.

Use place value understanding and properties of operations to add and subtract.
- Add within 100, including adding a two-digit and a one-digit number and adding multiples of tens to a two-digit number.
- Understand that in adding two-digit numbers, tens and tens are added, and ones and ones are added.
- Mentally find 10 more or 10 less than a given two-digit number.
- Subtract multiples of 10 in the range 10 to 90 from multiples of 10 in the same range.

Third Grade

Use place value understanding and properties of operations to perform multi-digit arithmetic.
- Round whole numbers to the nearest 10 or 100.
- Fluently add and subtract within 1,000.
- Multiply one-digit whole numbers by multiples of 10 from 10 to 90.

Number and Operations in Base Ten
Concepts Checklist

Concept		Date(s) Taught				

Place Value

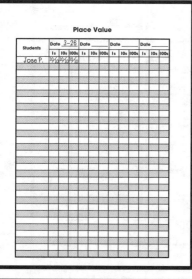

Use this form to track which students have mastered place value through the ones, tens, and hundreds and which students need extra practice or attention. First, record student names in the left-hand column. Take note of their progress as the unit is introduced, practiced, and concluded by writing grades, numbers right out of totals, or check marks. With all of your students' progress at a glance, you can plan lessons and assign group work efficiently.

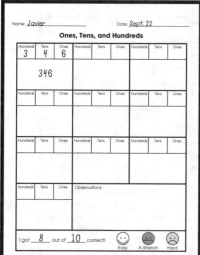

Allow students to show what they know about three-digit place value. You can either fill in the hundreds, tens, and ones spaces, or write a two- or three-digit number below. The student will either write the number or the place values for each digit. If working one on one with a student, you may give this number orally, adding another point of assessment.

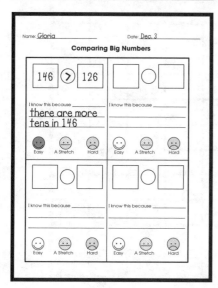

Once students have a working knowledge of three-digit place value, challenge them to compare numbers to 1,000. You or the students will fill in the two squares with two- or three-digit numbers. Students will fill in the circle with a comparison symbol. Students should be able to give reasons for their answers that compare the values of the digits in each number.

Place Value

Students	Date ____			Date ____			Date ____			Date ____		
	1s	10s	100s	1s	10s	100s	1s	10s	100s	1s	10s	100s

Ones, Tens, and Hundreds

Hundreds	Tens	Ones	Hundreds	Tens	Ones	Hundreds	Tens	Ones

Hundreds	Tens	Ones	Hundreds	Tens	Ones	Hundreds	Tens	Ones

Hundreds	Tens	Ones	Hundreds	Tens	Ones	Hundreds	Tens	Ones

Hundreds	Tens	Ones	Observations

I got _____ out of _____ correct!

Easy   A Stretch   Hard

Name: _____   Date: _____

Comparing Big Numbers

I know this because _____

_____

_____.

 Easy   A Stretch   Hard

I know this because _____

_____

_____.

 Easy   A Stretch   Hard

I know this because _____

_____

_____.

 Easy   A Stretch   Hard

I know this because _____

_____

_____.

 Easy   A Stretch   Hard

Counting

Second-grade students need to be able to count by 1s, 2s, 5s, 10s, and 100s to 1,000. This form will help you track which students have mastered these skills. Record each student's name and place a check mark under each skill as a student masters it. A quick glance at the blank spots will allow you to pull out groups of students who may need extra help or practice. Use the *Notes* section to record any observations.

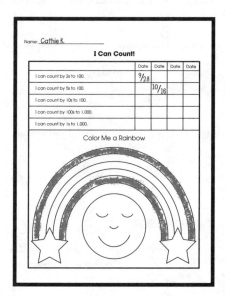

Students can keep track of the progress they make in learning to skip count and count to 1,000. When they have mastered one of the counting skills, they can record the date. To further reward progress, have students fill in one color of the rainbow for each skill mastered to show their successes. When the rainbow is complete, allow students to color the smiling face.

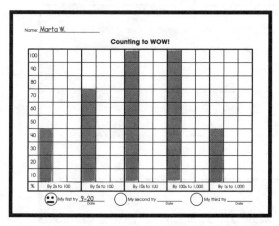

This sheet will allow students to track their counting skills over time. Have students record the results of three tries for each counting skill by filling in dates and coloring bars. After each try, students should fill in the circle with an expression to show how well they feel they did. This is also a good sheet to send along for practice at home. Ask students to have the family member they practice with initial the page.

Counting Assessment

✓ = Mastered Students	Counting to 1,000	Counting by 2s	Counting by 5s	Counting by 10s	Counting by 100s	Notes

Name: _____

I Can Count!

	Date	Date	Date	Date
I can count by 2s to 100.				
I can count by 5s to 100.				
I can count by 10s to 100.				
I can count by 100s to 1,000.				
I can count by 1s to 1,000.				

Color Me a Rainbow

Counting to WOW!

Name: _____

%	By 2s to 100	By 5s to 100	By 10s to 100	By 100s to 1,000	By 1s to 1,000
10					
20					
30					
40					
50					
60					
70					
80					
90					
100					

◯ My first try _____ Date

◯ My second try _____ Date

◯ My third try _____ Date

Numbers to 1,000

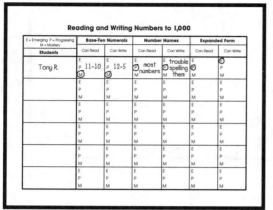

Second-grade students need to read and write base-ten numerals, number names, and expanded form. This sheet will help you track which parts of the unit(s) students mastered and which require more practice. Record student names in the left-hand column. As you present skills, circle E, P, or M to indicate progress. Use the remaining space to record dates of mastery or follow-up details. Use the notes when assigning groups or conducting conferences.

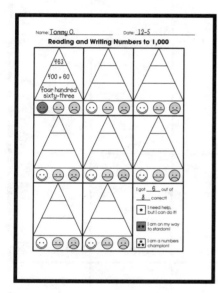

Use this sheet for one-on-one or group work. Have students fill in the pyramids starting at the top as you say a number. Have students write the number in the top triangle, followed by its expanded form and its number name. Have students color or circle the appropriate face below each problem. You will be able to see if students are still struggling by the eighth pyramid. The final square allows students to assess their work.

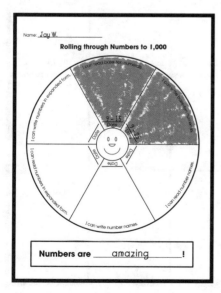

Ask students to keep this form to record their progress over time as they master number skills. They will date and color the appropriate piece of the circle as they master each skill. Once students have filled the color wheel, they can color the face in the center. Ask students to write a word or phrase to tell how they feel about numbers as they complete the page.

Reading and Writing Numbers to 1,000

E = Emerging P = Progressing M = Mastery	Base-Ten Numerals		Number Names		Expanded Form	
Students	Can Read	Can Write	Can Read	Can Write	Can Read	Can Write
	E P M	E P M	E P M	E P M	E P M	E P M
	E P M	E P M	E P M	E P M	E P M	E P M
	E P M	E P M	E P M	E P M	E P M	E P M
	E P M	E P M	E P M	E P M	E P M	E P M
	E P M	E P M	E P M	E P M	E P M	E P M
	E P M	E P M	E P M	E P M	E P M	E P M

Reading and Writing Numbers to 1,000

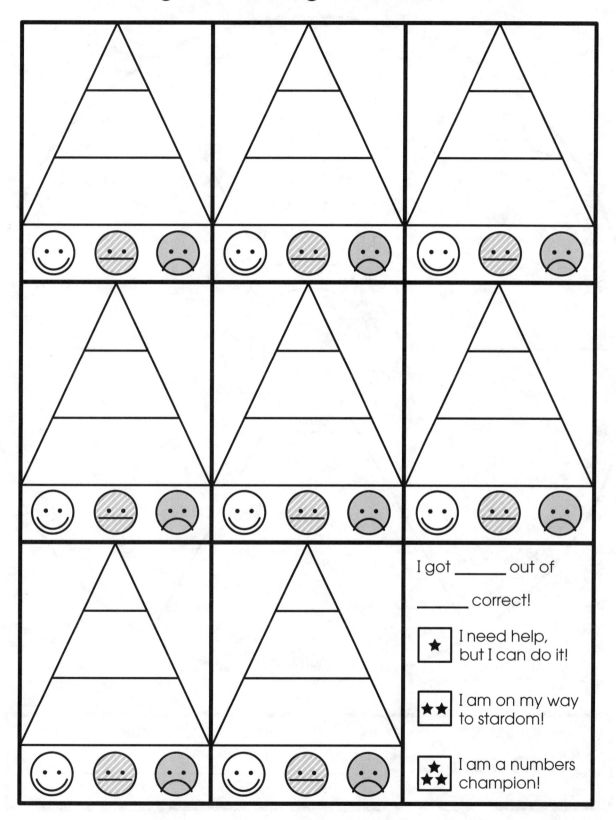

I got _____ out of _____ correct!

★ I need help, but I can do it!

★★ I am on my way to stardom!

★★★ I am a numbers champion!

Rolling through Numbers to 1,000

I can read base-ten numerals.

I can write numbers in expanded form.

I can write base-ten numerals.

I can write numbers in expanded form.

Date

Date

Date

Date

Date

I can read numbers in expanded form.

I can read number names.

I can write number names.

Numbers are _____!

Addition and Subtraction Fluency

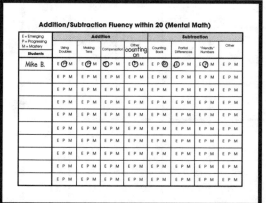

Various strategies can be used to teach students addition and subtraction fluency. Use this form to track student mastery of the strategies noted or add another strategy you are teaching. Record student names in the left-hand column. As a strategy is introduced and practiced, simply record the level of mastery by circling *E, P,* or *M.* If you want to use the sheet for additional assessments, use a different color of pen each time you circle levels of mastery.

This is a perfect sheet to show a student's progress over time. It's simple and will tell a lot at a glance. Each time you assess a student's ability to add and/or subtract fluently, simply write the date and how many problems were correct out of the total. Use the remaining space for notes about important observations or follow-up thoughts. This sheet is versatile; you can easily adapt it to record data in other curriculum areas by eliminating or changing the title.

This sheet gives students a simple way to show what they know about adding or subtracting 10 or 100 from numbers mentally. First, write numbers in the left-hand column or dictate them. Students must then fill in the sheet as quickly as possible. The bottom-left section allows students to score themselves. In the bottom right section, students should circle how well they think they did, from poorly (one star) to excellent (three stars).

Addition/Subtraction Fluency within 20 (Mental Math)

E = Emerging
P = Progressing
M = Mastery

Students	Addition				Subtraction			
	Using Doubles	Making Tens	Compensation	Other	Counting Back	Partial Differences	"Friendly" Numbers	Other
	E P M	E P M	E P M	E P M	E P M	E P M	E P M	E P M
	E P M	E P M	E P M	E P M	E P M	E P M	E P M	E P M
	E P M	E P M	E P M	E P M	E P M	E P M	E P M	E P M
	E P M	E P M	E P M	E P M	E P M	E P M	E P M	E P M
	E P M	E P M	E P M	E P M	E P M	E P M	E P M	E P M
	E P M	E P M	E P M	E P M	E P M	E P M	E P M	E P M
	E P M	E P M	E P M	E P M	E P M	E P M	E P M	E P M
	E P M	E P M	E P M	E P M	E P M	E P M	E P M	E P M
	E P M	E P M	E P M	E P M	E P M	E P M	E P M	E P M
	E P M	E P M	E P M	E P M	E P M	E P M	E P M	E P M
	E P M	E P M	E P M	E P M	E P M	E P M	E P M	E P M
	E P M	E P M	E P M	E P M	E P M	E P M	E P M	E P M

Name: _____

Addition and Subtraction Fluency

Date	Number correct
	Number completed

Date	Number correct
	Number completed

Date	Number correct
	Number completed

Date	Number correct
	Number completed

Date	Number correct
	Number completed

Date	Number correct
	Number completed

Date	Number correct
	Number completed

Date	Number correct
	Number completed

Date	Number correct
	Number completed

Date	Number correct
	Number completed

Name: _____ Date: _____

Mental Math

Numbers	+10	-10	+100	-100

I got _____ out of _____ correct!	How I Am Doing		
	☆	☆☆	☆☆☆

Addition and Subtraction to 1,000

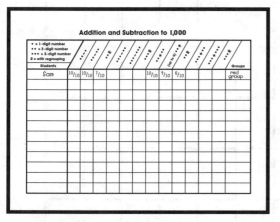

This form shows a lot of data at a glance. Record student names in the left-hand column. Each column to the right allows you to record scores, use check marks, or use your own scoring system. Please note the symbol key for the column headers, which cover addition and subtraction of two- and three-digit numbers, with and without regrouping. Use the right-hand column to assign groups as needed or for recording brief notes.

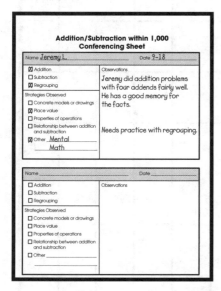

This conference sheet will make it easy for you to note a student's level of progress. Attach copies of this conference sheet to a clipboard for ease in taking notes on spot observations you make during classroom work. Check off the boxes that apply in the two left-hand boxes. Then, fill in the observation section with strengths or areas of need.

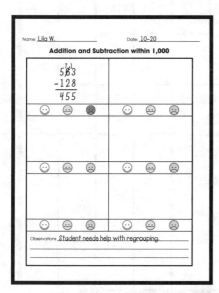

Use this sheet with individual students, small groups, or the whole class. Give addition or subtraction problems orally or write them on the board. Students should record one in a block, solve it, and then color or circle the face that shows how they felt about the problem (easy, a stretch, or hard). After the page is complete, make notes of your observations at the bottom of the sheet.

Addition and Subtraction to 1,000

Students	● − ● ●	● ● − ● ●	● ● R	● ● − ● ● ●	● ● ● − ● ● ●	● ● ● R	● ● + ● ●	● ● + ● ● (up to 4)	● ● R	● ● + ● ● ●	● ● ● + ● ● ●	● ● ● R	Groups

● = 1-digit number
● ● = 2-digit number
● ● ● = 3-digit number
R = with regrouping

Addition/Subtraction within 1,000
Conference Sheet

Name _____ Date _____

☐ Addition

☐ Subtraction

☐ Regrouping

Strategies Observed

☐ Concrete models or drawings

☐ Place value

☐ Properties of operations

☐ Relationship between addition
  and subtraction

☐ Other _____

_____

Observations

Name _____ Date _____

☐ Addition

☐ Subtraction

☐ Regrouping

Strategies Observed

☐ Concrete models or drawings

☐ Place value

☐ Properties of operations

☐ Relationship between addition
  and subtraction

☐ Other _____

_____

Observations

Addition and Subtraction within 1,000

Observations _____

_____

_____

Measurement and Data
Standards Crosswalk

First Grade

Measure lengths indirectly and by iterating length units.
- Compare and order three objects by length.
- Express the length of an object as a whole number of length units.
- Understand that length units must be the same size and have no gaps or overlaps.

Tell and write time.
- Tell and write time in hours and half hours using analog and digital clocks.

Represent and interpret data.
- Organize, represent, and interpret data with up to three categories.
- Ask and answer questions such as the total number represented, how many in each category, and differences between categories.

Third Grade

Solve problems involving measurement and estimation of intervals of time, liquid volumes, and masses of objects.
- Tell and write time to the nearest minute.
- Measure time intervals in minutes.
- Solve word problems involving addition and subtraction of time intervals in minutes.
- Measure and estimate liquid volume and mass using grams, kilograms, and liters.
- Solve volume and mass word problems given in the same units.

Represent and interpret data.
- Draw scaled picture and bar graphs to represent several categories.
- Analyze graphs to solve one- and two-step problems.
- Measure lengths to halves and fourths of an inch.
- Show fractional measurement data by creating line plots.

Geometric measurement: understand concepts of area and relate area to multiplication and addition.
- Recognize area as an attribute of plane figures.
- Understand the concept of a square unit.
- Find area by counting unit squares and laying square units side by side without gaps or overlaps.
- Relate area to the operations of multiplication and addition in real-world problems, using tiling and area models.
- Find areas of rectilinear figures by dividing them into nonoverlapping rectangles and adding the areas of the rectangles.

Geometric measurement: recognize perimeter as an attribute of plane figures and distinguish between linear and area measures.
- Find perimeters of polygons.
- Use perimeter to find unknown side lengths.
- Exhibit rectangles with the same perimeter and different areas or vice versa.

Measurement and Data
Concepts Checklist

	Concept	Date(s) Taught				

46

© Carson-Dellosa • CD-104918

Measurement Skills

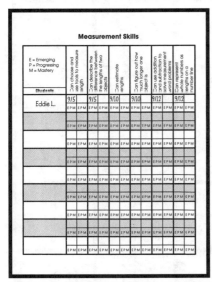

This is an ideal form to use for pretesting and posttesting. Record student names in the left-hand column. Use the blank space below the six measurement skills to date and rate student progress. Write the date in the blank space and circle *E*, *P*, or *M*. This form will allow you to see group progress at a glance.

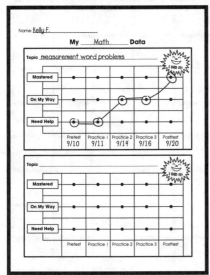

This student sheet will allow students to graph their progress over time. It is clear and simple. The form is also versatile; the title can be filled in to fit the lesson. Students will mark their progress from pretest to posttest by circling the appropriate dot and then connecting each consecutive level. The goal is to finally connect with the smiling character at the top right.

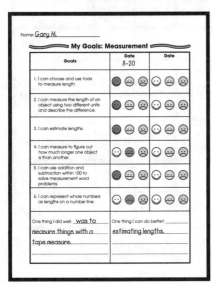

This *I can* sheet is for students to rate their progress in reaching goals in a measurement unit. There are two opportunities for them to master a skill. They should write the date the first time they assess themselves and then color or circle the appropriate face. They will fill in the second column at another date. Then, they should take time to reflect on the unit and write about one thing they did well and one thing they think they can do better.

Measurement Skills

E = Emerging P = Progressing M = Mastery **Students**	Can choose and use tools to measure length		Can describe the difference between the lengths of two objects		Can estimate lengths		Can figure out how much longer one object is		Can use addition and subtraction to solve measurement word problems		Can represent whole numbers as lengths on a number line	
	E P M	E P M	E P M	E P M	E P M	E P M	E P M	E P M	E P M	E P M	E P M	E P M
	E P M	E P M	E P M	E P M	E P M	E P M	E P M	E P M	E P M	E P M	E P M	E P M
	E P M	E P M	E P M	E P M	E P M	E P M	E P M	E P M	E P M	E P M	E P M	E P M
	E P M	E P M	E P M	E P M	E P M	E P M	E P M	E P M	E P M	E P M	E P M	E P M
	E P M	E P M	E P M	E P M	E P M	E P M	E P M	E P M	E P M	E P M	E P M	E P M
	E P M	E P M	E P M	E P M	E P M	E P M	E P M	E P M	E P M	E P M	E P M	E P M
	E P M	E P M	E P M	E P M	E P M	E P M	E P M	E P M	E P M	E P M	E P M	E P M
	E P M	E P M	E P M	E P M	E P M	E P M	E P M	E P M	E P M	E P M	E P M	E P M
	E P M	E P M	E P M	E P M	E P M	E P M	E P M	E P M	E P M	E P M	E P M	E P M

Name: _____

My _____ Data

Topic _____

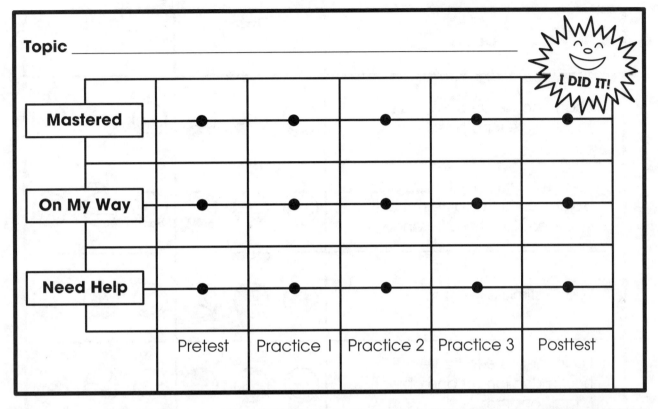

	Pretest	Practice 1	Practice 2	Practice 3	Posttest
Mastered	●	●	●	●	●
On My Way	●	●	●	●	●
Need Help	●	●	●	●	●

I DID IT!

Topic _____

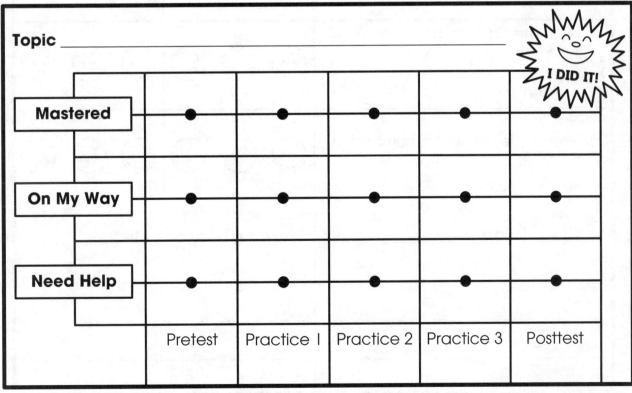

	Pretest	Practice 1	Practice 2	Practice 3	Posttest
Mastered	●	●	●	●	●
On My Way	●	●	●	●	●
Need Help	●	●	●	●	●

I DID IT!

Name: _____

My Goals: Measurement

Goals	Date	Date
1. I can choose and use tools to measure length.	☺ ☻ ☹	☺ ☻ ☹
2. I can measure the length of an object using two different units and describe the difference.	☺ ☻ ☹	☺ ☻ ☹
3. I can estimate lengths.	☺ ☻ ☹	☺ ☻ ☹
4. I can measure to figure out how much longer one object is than another.	☺ ☻ ☹	☺ ☻ ☹
5. I can use addition and subtraction within 100 to solve measurement word problems.	☺ ☻ ☹	☺ ☻ ☹
6. I can represent whole numbers as lengths on a number line.	☺ ☻ ☹	☺ ☻ ☹

One thing I did well: _____

_____

_____

_____

One thing I can do better: _____

_____

_____

_____

Time and Money

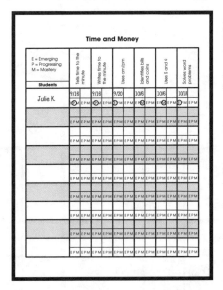

This is an ideal form to use for pretesting and posttesting. Record each student's name in the left-hand column. Then, use the space below the time and money skills to date and rate student progress. Write the date in the blank space and circle *E*, *P*, or *M*. This form will allow you to show progress at a glance.

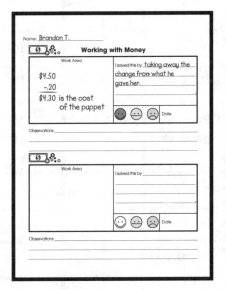

Allow students to show what they know about money. To test them, ask students to count out an amount of money; or, lay down some money and ask students to give you back an amount. Or, give students a written word problem. Have them first highlight or circle key words and then solve it. Attach the word problem to the sheet. Students should then explain their thinking process. Finally, have students date and rate their work by coloring or circling the appropriate face.

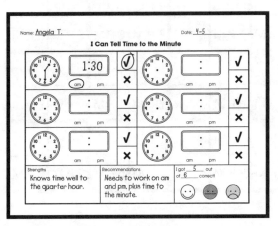

For each of six clock blocks, say a time and have students draw hands on the analog clock and write numbers on the digital clock. Give them a real-world scenario so that they can decide if the time is am or pm. Students can circle the check mark if they understand or the *X* if they don't understand. Fill in the *Strengths* and *Recommendations* sections and allow students to rate themselves.

Time and Money

E = Emerging P = Progressing M = Mastery **Students**	Tells time to the minute		Writes time to the minute		Uses am/pm		Identifies bills and coins		Uses $ and ¢		Solves word problems	
	E P M	E P M	E P M	E P M	E P M	E P M	E P M	E P M	E P M	E P M	E P M	E P M
	E P M	E P M	E P M	E P M	E P M	E P M	E P M	E P M	E P M	E P M	E P M	E P M
	E P M	E P M	E P M	E P M	E P M	E P M	E P M	E P M	E P M	E P M	E P M	E P M
	E P M	E P M	E P M	E P M	E P M	E P M	E P M	E P M	E P M	E P M	E P M	E P M
	E P M	E P M	E P M	E P M	E P M	E P M	E P M	E P M	E P M	E P M	E P M	E P M
	E P M	E P M	E P M	E P M	E P M	E P M	E P M	E P M	E P M	E P M	E P M	E P M
	E P M	E P M	E P M	E P M	E P M	E P M	E P M	E P M	E P M	E P M	E P M	E P M
	E P M	E P M	E P M	E P M	E P M	E P M	E P M	E P M	E P M	E P M	E P M	E P M
	E P M	E P M	E P M	E P M	E P M	E P M	E P M	E P M	E P M	E P M	E P M	E P M

Name: _____

Working with Money

Work Area	I solved this by _____
	_____
	_____
	_____
	_____ .

  Date

Observations _____

_____

Work Area	I solved this by _____
	_____
	_____
	_____
	_____ .

   Date

Observations _____

_____

_____

Name: _____

Date: _____

I Can Tell Time to the Minute

	✓	✗		✓	✗		✓	✗

am pm

am pm

am pm

am pm

am pm

am pm

Strengths

Recommendations

I got _____ out of _____ correct!

Representing Data

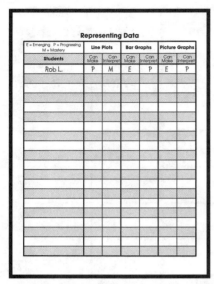

Second-grade students need to be able to make and interpret line plots, bar graphs, and picture graphs. Student mastery can be seen at a glance on this easy-to-use form. Write student names in the left-hand column. Use the key to mark each student's level of mastery as a unit progresses.

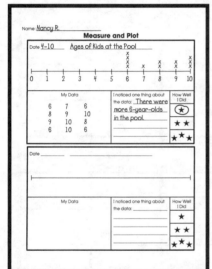

Allow students to show what they know about making line plots. Students should first consider what data they want to gather; the title should reflect this. Students can gather their data anywhere—at home, at school, or at the park—and record it under *My Data*. Students should mark their line plots to reflect their data. Then, they can write a sentence about what they concluded from looking at the data. Finally, they will give themselves a star rating to say how well they did on the project.

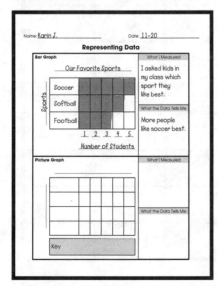

Use this form to assess whether students are able to make their own bar or picture graphs. You might want to begin by giving them the data to use for their first try. When they're ready, have them collect their own data. Students will need to fill in a title and label both axes before graphing the data. As a follow-up activity, students should write about what they measured and what the data concluded.

Representing Data

E = Emerging P = Progressing M = Mastery **Students**	**Line Plots**		**Bar Graphs**		**Picture Graphs**	
	Can Make	Can Interpret	Can Make	Can Interpret	Can Make	Can Interpret

Name: _____

Measure and Plot

Date _____   _____

|--|

My Data	I noticed one thing about the data: _____ _____ _____ _____ _____	How Well I Did
		★
		★ ★
		★★★

Date _____   _____

|--|

My Data	I noticed one thing about the data: _____ _____ _____ _____ _____	How Well I Did
		★
		★ ★
		★★★

Representing Data

Bar Graph

What I Measured

What the Data Tells Me

Picture Graph

Key

What I Measured

What the Data Tells Me

Geometry
Standards Crosswalk

First Grade
Geometry
Reason with shapes and their attributes.
- Distinguish between defining attributes and non-defining attributes.
- Build and draw shapes with defining attributes.
- Compose two-dimensional shapes (rectangles, squares, trapezoids, triangles, half circles, and quarter circles) or three-dimensional shapes (cubes, right rectangular prisms, right circular cones, and right circular cylinders) to create a composite shape, and compose new shapes from the composite shape.
- Partition circles and rectangles into two and four equal shares, using the words *halves*, *fourths*, and *quarters*, and the phrases *half of, fourth of,* and *quarter of* to describe the shares.
- Understand that decomposing a whole into equal shares creates smaller shares.

Third Grade
Number and Operations—Fractions
Develop understanding of fractions as numbers.
- Recognize fractions as equal parts of a whole.

Measurement and Data
Geometric measurement: understand concepts of area and relate area to multiplication and to addition.
- Recognize area as an attribute of plane figures.
- Understand the concept of a square unit.
- Find area by counting unit squares and laying square units side by side without gaps or overlaps.

Geometry
Reason with shapes and their attributes.
- Understand that shapes in different categories may share attributes and that the shared attributes can define a larger category.
- Recognize rhombuses, rectangles, and squares as examples of quadrilaterals and draw examples of quadrilaterals that do not belong to any of these subcategories.
- Partition shapes into parts with equal areas.
- Express the area of each part of a partition as a unit fraction of the whole.

Geometry Concepts Checklist

Concept		Date(s) Taught				

Shapes

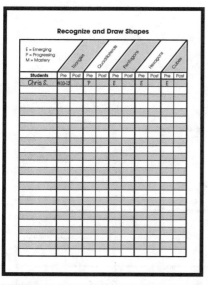

This form is perfect for tracking which students can recognize and draw triangles, quadrilaterals, pentagons, hexagons, and cubes. Record student names in the left column. Enter a level of mastery. Space allows for you to add the date of mastery if you wish. This will allow you to see at a glance which students have mastered these skills and which need help.

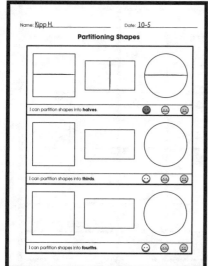

This sheet allows students to show what they know about partitioning shapes. They can complete each block independently by dividing each shape into halves, thirds, or fourths according to the *I can* statement. Students should return it after they have rated their progress by coloring or circling the appropriate face.

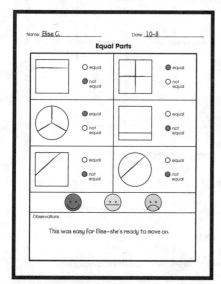

This form measures how well students understand the concepts of equal and not equal. Divide each shape into equal or unequal parts and ask students to mark each. If preferred, mark *equal* or *not equal* and ask students to partition the shapes accordingly. Then, students should color or circle the appropriate face. Use the observations section to record progress or follow-up needs.

Recognizing and Drawing Shapes

E = Emerging
P = Progressing
M = Mastery

Students	Triangles		Quadrilaterals		Pentagons		Hexagons		Cubes	
	Pre	Post	Pre	Post	Pre	Post	Pre	Post	Pre	Post

Partitioning Shapes

I can partition shapes into **halves**.

I can partition shapes into **thirds**.

I can partition shapes into **fourths**.

Equal Parts

○ equal

○ not equal

○ equal

○ not equal

○ equal

○ not equal

○ equal

○ not equal

○ equal

○ not equal

○ equal

○ not equal

Observations

Reading: Literature Standards Crosswalk

First Grade

Key Ideas and Details

- Ask and answer questions about key details in a text.
- Use key details to retell stories.
- Understand the message or lesson of a story.
- Use key details to describe characters, settings, and major events in a story.

Craft and Structure

- Identify words and phrases that suggest feelings or appeal to the senses.
- Explain differences between fiction and nonfiction books.
- Identify who is telling the story at various points in a text.

Integration of Knowledge and Ideas

- Use illustrations and details in a story to describe its characters, setting, or events.
- Compare and contrast the adventures and experiences of characters in stories.

Range of Reading and Level of Text Complexity

- Read prose and poetry of appropriate complexity for grade 1.

Third Grade

Key Ideas and Details

- Refer to text to ask and answer questions to demonstrate understanding.
- Recount stories, including fables, folktales, and myths from diverse cultures.
- Use key details to determine the central message, lesson, or moral in a text.
- Describe characters in a story and explain how their actions contribute to the sequence of events.

Craft and Structure

- Distinguish literal from nonliteral language when determining the meaning of words and phrases in a text.
- Refer to parts of stories, dramas, and poems when writing or speaking about a text, using terms such as *chapter*, *scene*, and *stanza*.
- Describe how each successive part of a story, drama, or poem builds on earlier sections.
- Distinguish their points of view from those of the narrator or characters.

Integration of Knowledge and Ideas

- Explain how its illustrations support what is conveyed in the text.
- Compare and contrast the themes, settings, and plots of stories written by the same author about the same or similar characters.

Range of Reading and Level of Text Complexity

- By the end of the year, read and comprehend literature independently at the high end of the grades 2 to 3 text complexity band.

Reading: Literature Concepts Checklist

	Concept	Date(s) Taught				

Reading Comprehension: Literature

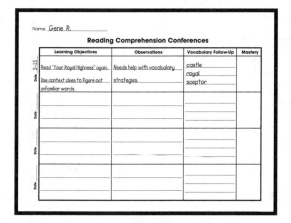

This form is ideal for student and parent conferences. When meeting with a student, decide on a learning objective, or goal, based on a current story the student is reading. You may choose the learning objective, but the student needs to understand it. Write and discuss the observations that made you choose this learning objective. Note a few vocabulary words that require study. Use a check mark to record mastery in the final column, plus any appropriate comments.

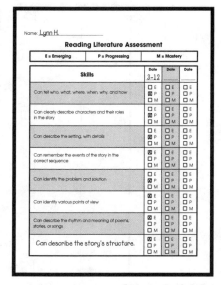

Use this form to keep track of student progress with the elements of reading comprehension. This will cover three assessments over time. Date the form at the top of the appropriate column. Using a simple check system, mark the student's level of mastery. Note: The last box has been left blank to allow you or the student to fill it in with any other skill.

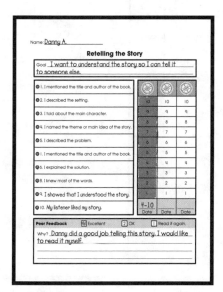

Students can use this form to assess their own progress on retelling three stories to peers. First, they should write a goal about retelling a story. This could range from remembering story order to making it interesting. Numbers 9 and 10 are blank to allow you or the student to add other specific skills. Peers should offer feedback by rating the storyteller and supporting the ratings with reasons. If a student tries this with three different peers, have the peer reviewers write with different colors of pens.

Reading Comprehension Conferences

Name: _____

Learning Objectives	Observations	Vocabulary Follow-Up	Mastery
Date			
Date			
Date			
Date			

Name: _____

Reading Literature: Assessment

E = Emerging	P = Progressing	M = Mastery	

Skills	Date ____	Date ____	Date ____
Can tell who, what, where, when, why, and how	☐ E ☐ P ☐ M	☐ E ☐ P ☐ M	☐ E ☐ P ☐ M
Can clearly describe characters and their roles in the story	☐ E ☐ P ☐ M	☐ E ☐ P ☐ M	☐ E ☐ P ☐ M
Can describe the setting, with details	☐ E ☐ P ☐ M	☐ E ☐ P ☐ M	☐ E ☐ P ☐ M
Can remember the events of the story in the correct sequence	☐ E ☐ P ☐ M	☐ E ☐ P ☐ M	☐ E ☐ P ☐ M
Can identify the problem and solution	☐ E ☐ P ☐ M	☐ E ☐ P ☐ M	☐ E ☐ P ☐ M
Can identify various points of view	☐ E ☐ P ☐ M	☐ E ☐ P ☐ M	☐ E ☐ P ☐ M
Can describe the rhythm and meaning of poems, stories, or songs	☐ E ☐ P ☐ M	☐ E ☐ P ☐ M	☐ E ☐ P ☐ M
	☐ E ☐ P ☐ M	☐ E ☐ P ☐ M	☐ E ☐ P ☐ M

Name: _____

Retelling the Story

Goal _____
_____

O 1. I mentioned the title and author of the book.			
O 2. I described the setting.	10	10	10
O 3. I told about the main character.	9	9	9
	8	8	8
O 4. I named the theme or main idea of the story.	7	7	7
O 5. I described the problem.	6	6	6
O 6. I mentioned the title and author of the book.	5	5	5
	4	4	4
O 7. I explained the solution.	3	3	3
O 8. I knew most of the words.	2	2	2
O 9.	1	1	1
O 10.	Date	Date	Date

Peer Feedback   3 Excellent   2 OK   1 Read it again.

Why? _____
_____
_____
_____

Reading Logs

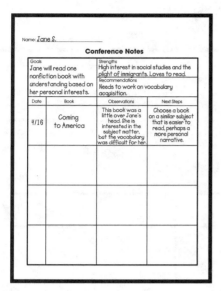

Use this form to confer with students about each completed fiction or nonfiction text. Write and discuss a goal with each student. Note the student's strengths and needs. Then, write the date of the conference and the name of the book that you discussed. In the *Observations* column, note 1) the student's reason for choosing the text; 2) the level of reading comprehension; 3) the ability to retell the story or recount facts; 4) the ability to summarize the reading; or 5) the areas of interest shown by the selection. Finally, plan and record the next steps or reading choices with the student.

Have students use this reading log to keep track of their independent reading. Have them write the title. After students have read self-selected books independently, they should note the date they read the books as well as their titles and authors. After coloring or circling an *E*, *J*, or *H*, students should write a brief opinion of the book and the amount of time spent reading it. Students should ask family members to initial each entry before returning the logs to school. The particulars of this form can be discussed at student reading conferences.

Have students use this pair of reading logs to keep track of their independent fiction or nonfiction reading. Each form should include the name of the book and its author or source as well as the date the student finished reading it. The top form asks for a brief synopsis of the story details in sequence. The bottom form asks for four fun facts learned from the book. Both forms ask students to rate the books by coloring or circling the appropriate face or checking an opinion.

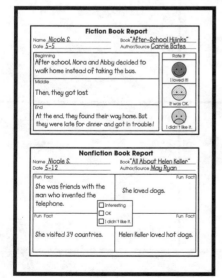

Name: _____

Conference Notes

Goals	Strengths		
	Recommendations		

Date	Book	Observations	Next Steps

Reading Log

Name: _____

My _____ (Fiction, Nonfiction)

Date	Title	Author				What I Think	Minutes Read	Parent Initials
			E	J	H			
			E	J	H			
			E	J	H			
			E	J	H			

E Easy   J Just Right   H Hard

Fiction Book Report

Name _____   Book _____

Date _____   Author/Source _____

Beginning	Rate It
	I loved it!
Middle	It was OK.
End	I didn't like it.

Nonfiction Book Report

Name _____   Book _____

Date _____   Author/Source _____

Fun Fact	Fun Fact

☐ Interesting
☐ OK
☐ I didn't like it.

Fun Fact	Fun Fact

Reading: Informational Text
Standards Crosswalk

First Grade

Key Ideas and Details

- Ask and answer questions about key details in a text.
- Identify the main topic and retell key details in a text.
- Connect two individuals, events, ideas, or pieces of information in a text.

Craft and Structure

- Ask and answer questions to help understand the meaning of words and phrases.
- Know and use text features (headings, tables of contents, glossaries, electronic menus, icons) to locate key facts or information in a text.
- Distinguish information provided by visual aids from that provided in a text.

Integration of Knowledge and Ideas

- Use the illustrations and details in a text to describe its key ideas.
- Identify the reasons an author gives to support points in a text.
- Identify basic similarities or differences between two texts on the same topic.

Range of Reading and Level of Text Complexity.

- Read informational texts that are appropriately complex for grade 1.

Third Grade

Key Ideas and Details

- Refer to text to ask and answer questions to demonstrate understanding.
- Determine the main idea of a text.
- Recount key details and explain how they support the main idea.
- Use appropriate language (time, sequence, cause and effect) to describe the relationship between a series of historic events, scientific ideas or concepts, or steps in technical procedures in a text.

Craft and Structure

- Determine the meaning of general academic and domain-specific words and phrases.
- Use text features and search tools to locate information.
- Distinguish their points of view from that of the author of a text.

Integration of Knowledge and Ideas

- Use information gained from illustrations and the words in a text to demonstrate understanding.
- Describe the logical connection between sentences and paragraphs in a text.
- Compare and contrast important points and key details from two texts on the same topic.

Range of Reading and Level of Text Complexity

- By the end of the year, read and comprehend informational texts at the high end of the grades 2 to 3 text complexity band independently and proficiently.

Reading: Informational Text
Concepts Checklist

Concept		Date(s) Taught				

Reading Comprehension: Informational Text

This form is ideal for tracking reading progress during the school year. Record student names in the left-hand column. Proceeding monthly, beginning in October, keep track of each student's reading level, using the scale that you are accustomed to. You may also use this form to group your students. This form is versatile; you can easily adapt it to record other subjects as well.

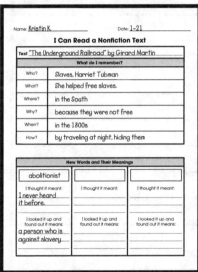

This form covers the essential elements of reading comprehension: the five W's and an H. Students will first write the title. Encourage students to add the author's name. To complete the top section, allow students to refer back to the text if they need help spelling any of the words, although you need not grade students on spelling. Do observe if they look back to the book to find answers. In the bottom section, have them write three words they did not know while reading the text and follow the directions in each section.

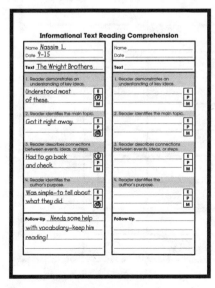

Have students use this form again and again for different books. Note that the level of mastery may not show progress from one reading to another if the books are of varying complexity. After writing the title of the book, ask questions to rate the student on four standards. Use the notes section below each column to record any observations. At the bottom of the form, note any follow-up thoughts.

Informational Text: Reading Levels

Students	October	November	December	January	February	March	April	May

I Can Read a Nonfiction Text

Text _____

What do I remember?	
Who?	
What?	
Where?	
Why?	
When?	
How?	

New Words and Their Meanings

I thought it meant:	I thought it meant:	I thought it meant:
I looked it up and found out it means:	I looked it up and found out it means:	I looked it up and found out it means:

Informational Text: Reading Comprehension

Name _____	Name _____
Date _____	Date _____

Text _____	Text _____

1. Reader demonstrates an understanding of key ideas.

_____ **E**
_____ **P**
                       M

2. Reader identifies the main topic.

_____ **E**
_____ **P**
                       M

3. Reader describes connections between events, ideas, or steps.

_____ **E**
_____ **P**
                       M

4. Reader identifies the author's purpose.

_____ **E**
_____ **P**
                       M

Follow-Up _____
_____
_____
_____

---

1. Reader demonstrates an understanding of key ideas.

_____ **E**
_____ **P**
                       M

2. Reader identifies the main topic.

_____ **E**
_____ **P**
                       M

3. Reader describes connections between events, ideas, or steps.

_____ **E**
_____ **P**
                       M

4. Reader identifies the author's purpose.

_____ **E**
_____ **P**
                       M

Follow-Up _____
_____
_____
_____

Text Features

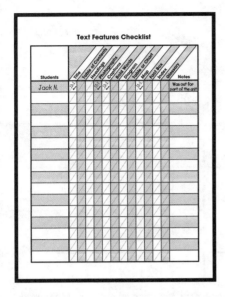

With this sheet, it is easy to track text features over time or in a unit. Record student names in the left-hand column. Twelve text features are listed. Below each feature, mark the date you taught the concept. If you taught the concept to the whole group, it is only necessary to mark the date on the first line. On the right side, use a marking system such as a simple check mark or *X* to indicate mastery. Use the last column to take notes or to add any other text features you focus on during the unit.

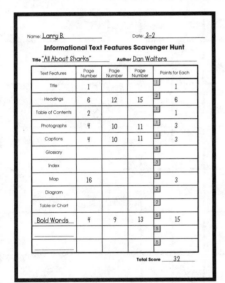

This sheet will serve as both an assessment and teaching tool for students. Have students look through a self-selected book for text features. First, they will write its title and author. As they page through the book, have them mark the page number each time they see a text feature. Then, they can take the number of points listed in the little boxes in the right-hand column and add to get a score for each line and then add to get a total score. Encourage students to try this again to see if they can beat their first scores.

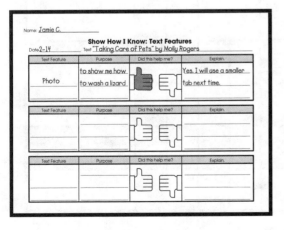

Have students choose a book with text features. As students read the book, they should take note of various text features and how they did with understanding of the text. Using this form, have students write the name and purpose of a text feature in the book. In the thumbs-up, thumbs-down section, they can color or circle their choice to indicate if they thought the text feature was helpful. They should explain why it did or did not help.

Text Features Checklist

Students	Title	Table of Contents	Headings	Photographs	Captions	Bold Words	Diagram	Table or Chart	Map	Fact Box	Index	Glossary	Notes

Name: _____   Date: _____

Informational Text Features Scavenger Hunt

Title _____   **Author** _____

Text Features	Page Number	Page Number	Page Number	Points for Each
Title				1
Headings				2
Table of Contents				1
Photographs				1
Captions				1
Glossary				3
Index				3
Map				3
Diagram				2
Table or Chart				2
_____				5
_____				5
_____				5

Total Score _____

Show How I Know: Text Features

Name: _____

Date _____

Text _____

Text Feature	Purpose	Did this help me?	Explain.

Reading: Foundational Skills Standards Crosswalk

First Grade

Print Concepts
- Recognize the unique first word, capitalization, and punctuation of a sentence.

Phonological Awareness
- Demonstrate understanding of spoken words, syllables, and phonemes.
- Distinguish long from short vowel sounds in spoken single-syllable words.
- Orally blend sounds, including consonant blends, in single-syllable words.
- Isolate and pronounce initial, medial vowel, and final sounds in spoken single-syllable words.
- Segment spoken single-syllable words into all individual sounds.

Phonics and Word Recognition
- Decode words using grade-level phonics and word analysis skills.
- Know the spelling and sounds of common consonant digraphs.
- Decode regularly spelled one-syllable words.
- Know final -*e* and other common vowel team long vowel sound patterns.
- Determine the number of syllables in a word by knowing that each syllable must have a vowel sound.
- Break words into known syllables to decode two-syllable words.
- Read words with inflectional endings.
- Recognize and read grade-appropriate irregularly spelled words.

Fluency
- Read with accuracy and fluency to support comprehension.
- Read grade-level text with purpose and understanding.
- Read grade-level text orally with accuracy, fluency, and expression.
- Use context and rereading to confirm or self-correct understanding of text.

Third Grade

Phonics and Word Recognition
- Decode words using grade-level phonics and word analysis skills.
- Identify and know the meanings of most common prefixes and suffixes.
- Decode words with common Latin suffixes.
- Decode multisyllabic words.
- Read grade-appropriate irregularly spelled words.

Fluency
- Read with sufficient accuracy and fluency to support comprehension.
- Read grade-level text with purpose and understanding.
- Read grade-level prose and poetry with accuracy, appropriate rate, and expression on successive readings.
- Use context and rereading to confirm or self-correct word recognition and understanding.

Reading: Foundational Skills Concepts Checklist

Concept		Date(s) Taught				

Vowel Sounds

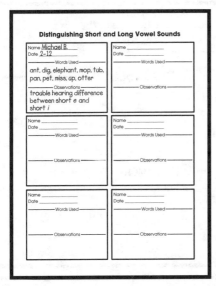

Use this form as you teach students to distinguish between short and long vowel sounds. Use this form to assess six different students or with one student for pretesting, practice, and posttesting over time. If for a single student, write the student name in one box only but date each assessment. Record which words you used to test or teach student(s). Then, note any observations that may be helpful for remediation.

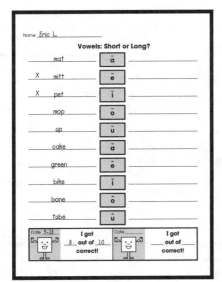

Use this form to assess students on their knowledge of short and long vowel sounds. Write words on cards or write them on the board for students to copy in the correct spaces. Provide immediate feedback so that students can date and rate themselves in the boxes at the bottom of the page. This sheet is intended to offer pretest and posttest results or to allow for two practice sessions.

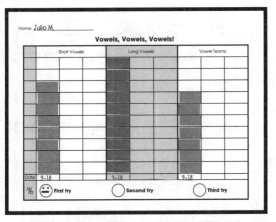

Use this form to show student progress in learning long and short vowels and vowel teams. Each column includes space for three tries. Complete the left-hand column using your own grading system, such as writing percentages or numbering from 1 to 10. Students will fill in the bars to match their scores. On each try, students should draw an appropriate face to show how they feel about their scores.

Distinguishing Short and Long Vowel Sounds

Name _____
Date _____
—————————Words Used—————————

—————————Observations—————————

Name _____
Date _____
—————————Words Used—————————

—————————Observations—————————

Name _____
Date _____
—————————Words Used—————————

—————————Observations—————————

Name _____
Date _____
—————————Words Used—————————

—————————Observations—————————

Name _____
Date _____
—————————Words Used—————————

—————————Observations—————————

Name _____
Date _____
—————————Words Used—————————

—————————Observations—————————

Name: _____

Vowels: Short or Long?

_____	ă	_____
_____	ĕ	_____
_____	ĭ	_____
_____	ŏ	_____
_____	ŭ	_____
_____	ā	_____
_____	ē	_____
_____	ī	_____
_____	ō	_____
_____	ū	_____

Date _____   **I got ____ out of ____ correct!**

Date _____   **I got ____ out of ____ correct!**

Name: _____

Vowels, Vowels, Vowels, Vowels!

Short Vowels			Long Vowels			Vowel Teams		

Date

%

○ First try   ○ Second try   ○ Third try

90

Spelling

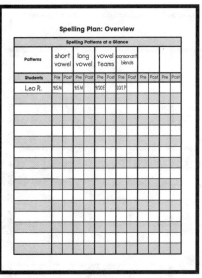

This is an ideal form to use for pretesting and posttesting. Record student names in the left-hand column. In the *Patterns* row, write spelling patterns you are teaching. Use the spaces below to date and rate student progress. Use a check mark or other rating system to indicate mastery. This form will allow you to see a student's progress or that of the entire class at a glance.

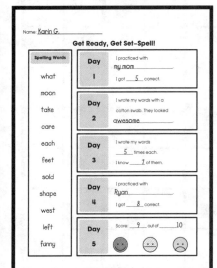

If you distribute weekly spelling lists on Monday, this form offers the student not only the list of spelling words but also four different options for practice. Either you or the student will write the week's spelling words in the left-hand column. Then, students will complete each day's option throughout the week. On Day 5, students get to post their scores. They should color or circle the face that tells how they feel about their spelling scores.

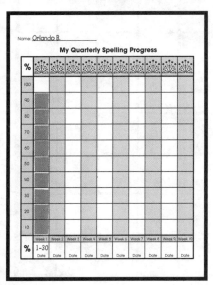

This form will highlight a student's spelling progress across 10 weeks or one quarter. It is a very simple sheet that students can fill out themselves after they get their spelling test scores. Convert their scores into percentages (if that is not your usual way of grading) for the purpose of this graph. Regularly check with students to see how they feel about their progress. This sheet will allow you to troubleshoot if you notice a sudden dip in scores.

Spelling Plan: Overview

Spelling Patterns at a Glance													
Patterns													
Students	Pre	Post	Pre	Post	Pre	Post	Pre	Post	Pre	Post	Pre	Post

Name: _____

Get Ready, Get Set—Spell!

Spelling Words

Day 1

I practiced with

_____.

I got _____ correct.

Day 2

I wrote my words with a

cotton swab. They looked

_____.

Day 3

I wrote my words

_____ times each.

I know _____ of them.

Day 4

I practiced with

_____.

I got _____ correct.

Day 5

Score: _____ out of _____

My Quarterly Spelling Progress

%										
100										
90										
80										
70										
60										
50										
40										
30										
20										
10										
	Week 1	Week 2	Week 3	Week 4	Week 5	Week 6	Week 7	Week 8	Week 9	Week 10
%										
	Date	Date	Date	Date	Date	Date	Date	Date	Date	Date

Prefixes and Suffixes

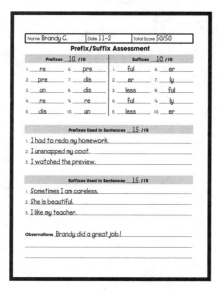

Reproduce this sheet to pretest and posttest. Or, make copies to use for multiple assessments. Complete these with individual students or as a class. Write two to three prefixes or suffixes on the board. Then, say or show a word so that students can find the prefix or suffix. The sheet includes space for them to write 10 of each. But, at the beginning of a unit, you may wish to offer only a few of one or both types of affixes. Students will then use three words from each section in sentences. Record any observations at the bottom of the sheet.

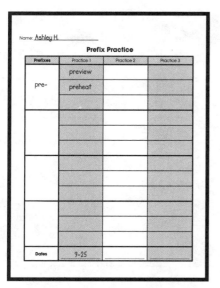

Use this simple practice sheet three times to show progress throughout the prefix unit. Write prefixes in the left-hand column. Students will then write words that begin with that prefix in the second column. You need not grade students on their spelling other than that of the prefixes. Instead, monitor their understanding of the prefixes and their uses.

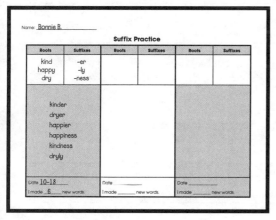

This sheet helps student show progress with roots and suffixes. Use it three times to show progress through the suffix unit. Complete the roots and suffixes boxes with up to four roots and suffixes or write them on the board for students to copy. Students will then make new words by combining one root with one suffix. After receiving your feedback, students should write the date and rate their success. You need not grade students on their spelling.

Prefix/Suffix Assessment

| Prefixes _____ /10 | Suffixes _____ /10 |

1. _____   6. _____   1. _____   6. _____

2. _____   7. _____   2. _____   7. _____

3. _____   8. _____   3. _____   8. _____

4. _____   9. _____   4. _____   9. _____

5. _____   10. _____   5. _____   10. _____

Prefixes Used in Sentences _____ /15

1. _____

2. _____

3. _____

Suffixes Used in Sentences _____ /15

1. _____

2. _____

3. _____

Observations _____

_____

_____

Name: _____

Prefix Practice

Prefixes	Practice 1	Practice 2	Practice 3
Dates			

Suffix Practice

Name: _____

Roots	Suffixes

Date _____
I made _____ new words.

Roots	Suffixes

Date _____
I made _____ new words.

Roots	Suffixes

Date _____
I made _____ new words.

Vocabulary

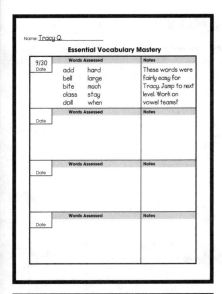

Use this form to track the vocabulary words assigned to individual students during individual or group practice sessions. Assess students' ability to read the words on their handwritten lists or on flash cards. Mark the words that students mastered. Take notes on observed problem areas or successful learning strategies. When a student is ready, assign a new set of words.

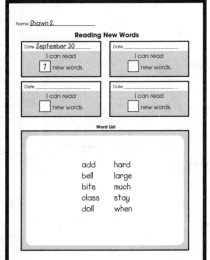

Students will use this form to record their assigned vocabulary in the *Word List* box. Allow time for students to practice these words with partners and record each new level of success. Use this sheet with any new vocabulary assignment for up to four practice sessions.

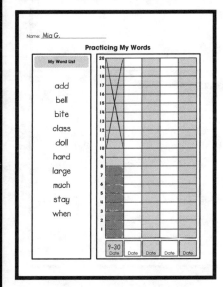

This form is perfect to show students the progress they have made with new vocabulary. Students will write their assigned words in the *My Word List* section on the left. The bar graph to the right has five bars to be used for five days of the school week or five random practices or assessments. Students may want to mark the bar, which goes to 20, where their assigned word lists stop; otherwise, it may appear that they did not do as well as they actually did. Students should fill in each date and compare levels of progress.

Name: _____

Essential Vocabulary Mastery

Date	Words Assessed	Notes

Date	Words Assessed	Notes

Date	Words Assessed	Notes

Date	Words Assessed	Notes

Name: _____

Reading New Words

Date _____

I can read

[ ] new words.

Date _____

I can read

[ ] new words.

Date _____

I can read

[ ] new words.

Date _____

I can read

[ ] new words.

Word List

Name: _____

Practicing My Words

My Word List

20				
19				
18				
17				
16				
15				
14				
13				
12				
11				
10				
9				
8				
7				
6				
5				
4				
3				
2				
1				
Date	Date	Date	Date	Date

Fluency

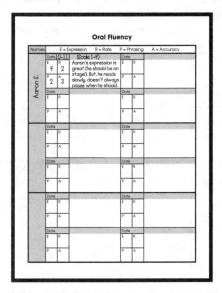

This form allows you to pinpoint progress in the four main elements of oral fluency. Give a student a short passage to read on four different occasions. Record student names in the far left column. Each student's area has four rectangles for assessment. Date one each time a student reads a passage. Below, in the boxes labeled *E*, *R*, *P*, and *A*, use your preferred rating scale. Use the note section to record any observations. The form allows you to rate fluency four times for each student, making the level of progress (or lack of progress) apparent.

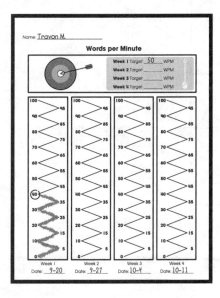

Fluency standards vary, but most will agree that a second-grade student should be reading 50 to 100 words per minute. Rates should rise throughout the school year. This sheet will help you and your students track their fluency progress. After a trial assessment, set a goal for the next reading that is slightly higher. Write the number on the top right. After the student has read a grade-level passage for a minute, have him circle the number of words read and color the path from 0 to it. Do this for four consecutive weeks to chart student progress.

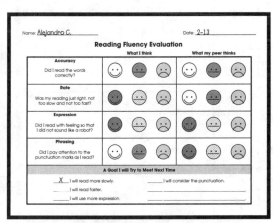

Fluent readers can recognize sight words automatically, which is critical to reading comprehension. This form allows students to check on their reading fluency. Pair students to read together. Then, have the reader rate himself by coloring or circling an appropriate face. The peer will rate the reader on the same points. Encourage pairs to discuss any discrepancies between ratings. Finally, students should set goals for the next time.

Oral Fluency

Names	E = Expression	R = Rate	P = Phrasing	A = Accuracy

	Date			Date		
	E	R		E	R	
	P	A		P	A	
	Date			Date		
	E	R		E	R	
	P	A		P	A	
	Date			Date		
	E	R		E	R	
	P	A		P	A	
	Date			Date		
	E	R		E	R	
	P	A		P	A	
	Date			Date		
	E	R		E	R	
	P	A		P	A	
	Date			Date		
	E	R		E	R	
	P	A		P	A	

Name: _____

Words per Minute

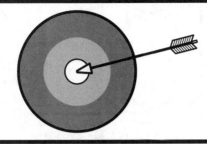

| Week 1 Target _____ WPM |
| Week 2 Target _____ WPM |
| Week 3 Target _____ WPM |
| Week 4 Target _____ WPM |

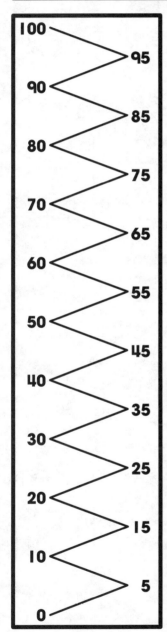

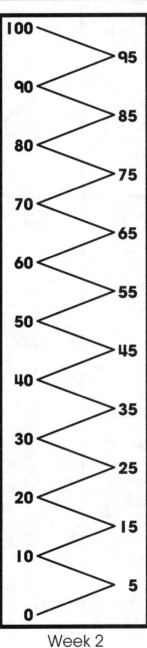

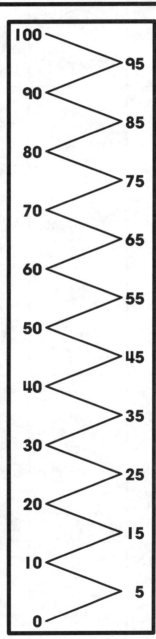

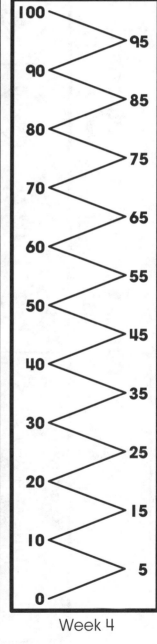

Week 1

Week 2

Week 3

Week 4

Date: _____

Date: _____

Date: _____

Date: _____

Name: _____

Date: _____

Reading Fluency Evaluation

	What I think			What my peer thinks		
Accuracy Did I read the words correctly?	☺	◑	☹	☺	◑	☹
Rate Was my reading just right, not too slow and not too fast?	☺	◑	☹	☺	◑	☹
Expression Did I read with feeling so that I did not sound like a robot?	☺	◑	☹	☺	◑	☹
Phrasing Did I pay attention to the punctuation marks as I read?	☺	◑	☹	☺	◑	☹

A Goal I will Try to Meet Next Time

_____ I will read more slowly.

_____ I will read faster.

_____ I will use more expression.

_____ I will consider the punctuation.

_____ _____

Writing Standards Crosswalk

First Grade

Text Types and Purposes
- Write an opinion piece on a topic or book, and provide a reason and a closing.
- Write informative/explanatory text that includes a topic, facts, and a closing.
- Write a narrative recounting two or more sequenced events that uses details and order words, and provides a closing.

Production and Distribution of Writing

With guidance and support:
- Focus on a topic, respond to peer feedback, and add details to strengthen writing.
- Use a variety of digital tools to produce and publish writing, including with peers.

Research to Build and Present Knowledge
- Participate in shared research and writing projects.
- With guidance and support, recall or gather information to answer a question.

Third Grade

Text Types and Purposes
- Write opinion pieces, supporting a point of view with reasons.
- Introduce a topic or text, state an opinion, and list reasons in an organized manner; use linking words and phrases; provide a concluding statement or section.
- Write texts to examine a topic and convey ideas and information clearly.
- Introduce a topic, group related information, and include illustrations when useful; develop the topic with facts, definitions, and details; use linking words and phrases to connect ideas; and provide a concluding statement or section.
- Write narratives using effective techniques, details, and clear sequences.
- Establish a situation and introduce a narrator and/or characters; organize a natural event sequence; use dialogue; describe the actions, thoughts, and feelings of characters; use temporal words and phrases to signal event order; provide closure.

Production and Distribution of Writing

With guidance and support:
- Develop, organize, and produce writing appropriate to task and purpose.
- Develop and strengthen writing by planning, revising, and editing.
- Use technology to produce and publish writing (using keyboarding skills), including in collaboration with others.

Research to Build and Present Knowledge
- Conduct research to build knowledge about a topic.
- Recall information or gather information from print and digital sources.
- Take brief notes on sources and sort evidence into provided categories.

Range of Writing
- Routinely write for a range of discipline-specific tasks, purposes, and audiences.

Writing Concepts Checklist

Concept		Date(s) Taught				

Opinion Writing

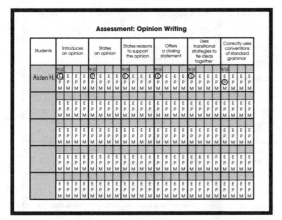

This is an ideal sheet to track students' writing proficiencies. You may also easily modify the sheet to track other types of writing. Record each student's name in the left-hand column. Under each skill are four spaces for recording dates of different writing work. Record the date and circle the level of progress. With this information at your fingertips, you can track students' progress over time, as well as their strengths and need.

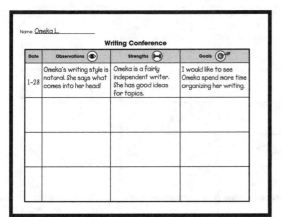

Begin writing conferences with positive affirmations of what students do well, statements of strengths to build on, and goals for upcoming writing projects. Record the date in the left-hand column. Write comments and observations in the subsequent columns. These comments and copies of the writing will be helpful at end-of-the-year conferences.

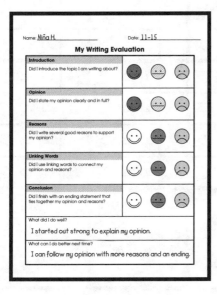

This is an ideal sheet for students to use many times with various writing projects. Students can use it to organize their work, as well as to check their writing when finished. Students will color or circle a face next to each skill to show if they were successful. In the bottom two boxes, students should write short statements about something they did well and something they can do better next time.

Assessment: Opinion Writing

Students	Introduces an opinion	States an opinion	States reasons to support the opinion	Offers a closing statement	Uses transitional strategies to tie ideas together	Correctly uses conventions of standard grammar
	E P M	E P M	E P M	E P M	E P M	E P M
	E P M	E P M	E P M	E P M	E P M	E P M
	E P M	E P M	E P M	E P M	E P M	E P M
	E P M	E P M	E P M	E P M	E P M	E P M
	E P M	E P M	E P M	E P M	E P M	E P M
	E P M	E P M	E P M	E P M	E P M	E P M
	E P M	E P M	E P M	E P M	E P M	E P M
	E P M	E P M	E P M	E P M	E P M	E P M
	E P M	E P M	E P M	E P M	E P M	E P M
	E P M	E P M	E P M	E P M	E P M	E P M
	E P M	E P M	E P M	E P M	E P M	E P M
	E P M	E P M	E P M	E P M	E P M	E P M
	E P M	E P M	E P M	E P M	E P M	E P M
	E P M	E P M	E P M	E P M	E P M	E P M
	E P M	E P M	E P M	E P M	E P M	E P M
	E P M	E P M	E P M	E P M	E P M	E P M
	E P M	E P M	E P M	E P M	E P M	E P M
	E P M	E P M	E P M	E P M	E P M	E P M
	E P M	E P M	E P M	E P M	E P M	E P M
	E P M	E P M	E P M	E P M	E P M	E P M

Name: _____

Writing Conference

Date	Observations 👁	Strengths 🔩	Goals 🎯

Name: _____   Date: _____

My Writing Evaluation

Introduction Did I introduce the topic I am writing about?	
Opinion Did I state my opinion clearly and in full?	
Reasons Did I write several good reasons to support my opinion?	
Linking Words Did I use linking words to connect my opinion and reasons?	
Conclusion Did I finish with an ending statement that ties together my opinion and reasons?	

What did I do well?

What can I do better next time?

Informative Writing

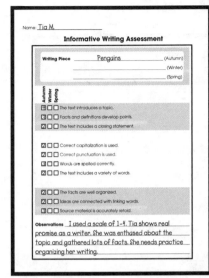

Use this sheet to track a student's progress, strengths, and weaknesses throughout the year. You may find it useful to attach copies of each piece of writing to the skill assessment sheet so that examples are at your fingertips. Write the name of each piece of writing at the top of the sheet. Mark your assessment of the student's writing skills by filling in the boxes with the rating scale of your choice. This sheet shows a scale of 1 to 4, with 4 being mastery. Make note of your observations at the bottom of the sheet. You may need to add another page of notes.

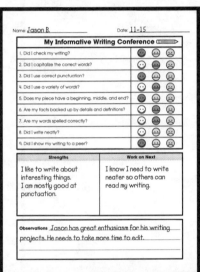

Use this form during a student writing conference regarding a particular piece of writing. Read the piece together and point out the good points and any errors. Then, allow the student to rate herself by coloring or circling the appropriate face. The student will also fill in the next two boxes by writing a sentence about what she has done well and what she can do better next time. Note any observations in the bottom section, including a compliment and a goal.

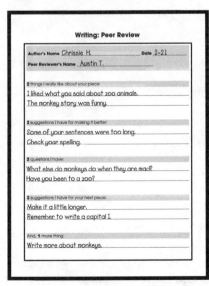

Peer reviews can be quite useful in helping students improve their work. Make sure to monitor sessions closely to ensure that students are respectful of each other's feelings. If accepted, this constructive peer feedback will help writers revise and improve their work. This sheet is for the peer reviewer to complete. It should include the author's name, date, and peer reviewer's name at the top. After reading the piece, the peer reviewer should complete the rest of the sheet with thoughtful and honest statements. For future reference, attach a copy of the writing to the peer review sheet.

Name: _____

Informative Writing Assessment

Writing Piece _____ (Autumn)

_____ (Winter)

_____ (Spring)

Autumn Winter Spring

☐ ☐ ☐ The text introduces a topic.

☐ ☐ ☐ Facts and definitions develop points.

☐ ☐ ☐ The text includes a closing statement.

☐ ☐ ☐ Correct capitalization is used.

☐ ☐ ☐ Correct punctuation is used.

☐ ☐ ☐ Words are spelled correctly.

☐ ☐ ☐ The text includes a variety of words.

☐ ☐ ☐ The facts are well organized.

☐ ☐ ☐ Ideas are connected with linking words.

☐ ☐ ☐ Source material is accurately retold.

Observations _____

_____

_____

_____

Name: _____   Date: _____

My Informative Writing Conference ✏️

1. Did I check my writing?	🙂	😐	🙁
2. Did I capitalize the correct words?	🙂	😐	🙁
3. Did I use correct punctuation?	🙂	😐	🙁
4. Did I use a variety of words?	🙂	😐	🙁
5. Does my piece have a beginning, middle, and end?	🙂	😐	🙁
6. Are my facts backed up by details and definitions?	🙂	😐	🙁
7. Are my words spelled correctly?	🙂	😐	🙁
8. Did I write neatly?	🙂	😐	🙁
9. Did I show my writing to a peer?	🙂	😐	🙁

Strengths	Work on Next

Observations _____

_____

_____

Writing: Peer Review

Author's Name _____ **Date** _____

Peer Reviewer's Name _____

2 things I really like about your piece:

_____

_____

2 suggestions I have for making it better:

_____

_____

2 questions I have:

_____

_____

2 suggestions I have for your next piece:

_____

_____

And, **1** more thing:

_____

Narrative Writing

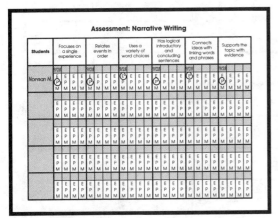

This is an ideal sheet to track students' growing writing skills. You can easily modify the sheet to track other types of writing. Record each student's name in the left column. Under each skill are four spaces for recording dates of different writing work. Record the date and circle the level of progress on that date. With this information at your fingertips, you can track students' progress, as well as their strengths and weaknesses.

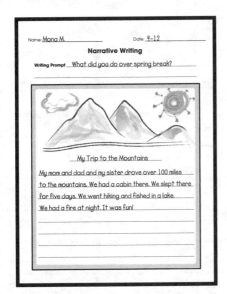

This is a good form to use to collect samples of student writing at different times throughout the year. You can write different writing prompts, or if used with the entire class, write your prompt on the board and ask students to copy it. Students will then write a story in response to the prompt and illustrate it. Some students may wish to make a drawing first and then write about the drawing.

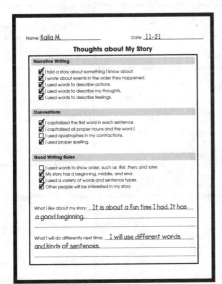

This form makes it easy for students to assess themselves on their narrative writing. After signing and dating the form, they need only check off the boxes of the skills they think they mastered with their narratives. You may also introduce this form before the writing lesson to remind students of the skills they should use. After checking off the appropriate boxes, have students write a sentence or two to tell what they like about their stories and what they will do differently next time.

Assessment: Narrative Writing

Students	Focuses on a single experience					Relates events in order					Uses a variety of word choices					Has logical introductory and concluding sentences					Connects ideas with linking words and phrases					Supports the topic with evidence				
	E P M	E P M	E P M	E P M	E P M	E P M	E P M	E P M	E P M	E P M	E P M	E P M	E P M	E P M	E P M	E P M	E P M	E P M	E P M	E P M	E P M	E P M	E P M	E P M	E P M	E P M	E P M	E P M	E P M	E P M
	E P M	E P M	E P M	E P M	E P M	E P M	E P M	E P M	E P M	E P M	E P M	E P M	E P M	E P M	E P M	E P M	E P M	E P M	E P M	E P M	E P M	E P M	E P M	E P M	E P M	E P M	E P M	E P M	E P M	E P M
	E P M	E P M	E P M	E P M	E P M	E P M	E P M	E P M	E P M	E P M	E P M	E P M	E P M	E P M	E P M	E P M	E P M	E P M	E P M	E P M	E P M	E P M	E P M	E P M	E P M	E P M	E P M	E P M	E P M	E P M
	E P M	E P M	E P M	E P M	E P M	E P M	E P M	E P M	E P M	E P M	E P M	E P M	E P M	E P M	E P M	E P M	E P M	E P M	E P M	E P M	E P M	E P M	E P M	E P M	E P M	E P M	E P M	E P M	E P M	E P M

Narrative Writing

Writing Prompt _____

_____

Thoughts about My Story

Narrative Writing

- ☐ I told a story about something I know about.
- ☐ I wrote about events in the order they happened.
- ☐ I used words to describe actions.
- ☐ I used words to describe my thoughts.
- ☐ I used words to describe feelings.

Conventions

- ☐ I capitalized the first word in each sentence.
- ☐ I capitalized all proper nouns and the word *I*.
- ☐ I used apostrophes in my contractions.
- ☐ I used proper spelling.

Good Writing Rules

- ☐ I used words to show order, such as *first*, *then*, and *later*.
- ☐ My story has a beginning, middle, and end.
- ☐ I used a variety of words and sentence types.
- ☐ Other people will be interested in my story.

What I like about my story: _____

_____

_____

What I will do differently next time: _____

_____

_____

Revising and Editing

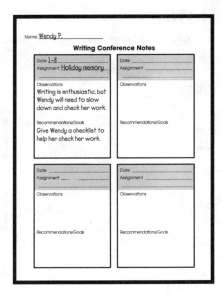

This form is specifically designed to record a broad overview of a student's revising and editing skills. Allow students to write a rough draft of a paragraph or text before conferencing. Read the rough draft together and then record your observations and recommendations. This sheet will cover four separate conferences. Time-Saving Tip: Print this page on large adhesive labels to easily attach to the back of student samples. Visit our website for the template.

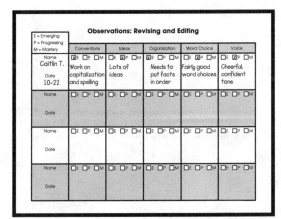

Use this form to fine-tune a student's revising and editing skills. Five specific skills are listed, with space to list other group or class members. Record individual names in the left column. Then, place a check mark in the appropriate level for each skill. Use the remaining space in the boxes for writing comments, which will be useful at conferences. If desired, attach writing samples to the back of these forms.

This sheet encourages students to write, edit, and revise a story. Students should write the title at the top, followed by a rough draft or finished version of the story. Next, have students pair with other students. Monitor the interactions to ensure that students are respectful of each other's feelings. Acceptable constructive feedback will help young writers improve their work. After reading the piece, the peer reviewer should circle *Y* for *yes* or *N* for *no* to answer the questions. Students can discuss any conflicting answers.

Writing Conference Notes

Date _____

Assignment _____

_____

Observations

Recommendations/Goals

Date _____

Assignment _____

_____

Observations

Recommendations/Goals

Date _____

Assignment _____

_____

Observations

Recommendations/Goals

Date _____

Assignment _____

_____

Observations

Recommendations/Goals

Observations: Revising and Editing

E = Emerging
P = Progressing
M = Mastery

	Conventions	Ideas	Organization	Word Choice	Voice
Name Date	□E □P □M	□E □P □M	□E □P □M	□E □P □M	□E □P □M
Name Date	□E □P □M	□E □P □M	□E □P □M	□E □P □M	□E □P □M
Name Date	□E □P □M	□E □P □M	□E □P □M	□E □P □M	□E □P □M
Name Date	□E □P □M	□E □P □M	□E □P □M	□E □P □M	□E □P □M

I Can Edit My Stories

My Story _____

_____

_____

_____

_____

_____

_____

_____

_____

Let's edit!

	Me		Peer	
Did I capitalize the first word of each sentence, proper names, titles, and *I*?	Y	N	Y	N
Did I use correct punctuation?	Y	N	Y	N
Do my nouns and verbs match?	Y	N	Y	N
Are all of the words spelled correctly?	Y	N	Y	N
Does my story make sense?	Y	N	Y	N

Speaking and Listening Standards Crosswalk

First Grade

Comprehension and Collaboration

- Participate in group discussions about grade-appropriate topics and texts.
- Follow agreed-upon discussion rules.
- Respond to remarks of others.
- Ask for clarification if needed.
- Ask and answer questions about key details in a text or other channels of information.
- Ask and answer questions about what a speaker says to better understand something.

Presentation of Knowledge and Ideas

- Use relevant details, ideas, and feelings to describe people, places, things, and events.
- Add visual displays to clarify descriptions when appropriate.

Third Grade

Comprehension and Collaboration

- Participate in collaborative discussions on grade 3 topics and texts.
- Prepare for discussions and participate appropriately.
- Follow agreed-upon discussion rules.
- Ask questions to clarify information presented, stay on topic, and offer relevant comments.
- Explain their ideas and understanding in light of a discussion.
- Determine the main ideas and supporting details of a text read aloud or multimedia presentations.
- Ask and answer questions about information from a speaker, offering appropriate elaboration.

Presentation of Knowledge and Ideas

- Speak clearly at an understandable pace to report on a topic or text, tell a story, or recount an experience with appropriate facts and descriptive details.
- Create audio recordings of stories or poems that demonstrate fluency and appropriate pacing.
- Add visual displays when needed to enhance certain facts or details.
- Speak in complete sentences when appropriate to provide requested detail or clarification.

Speaking and Listening Concepts Checklist

Concept		Date(s) Taught				

Interaction

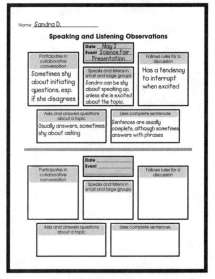

Use this form to track any kind of interaction: peer conversations, student presentations, and small- or large-group discussions. The top middle box allows you to differentiate between these events. One page offers two opportunities to observe the same student. Keep these forms on a clipboard as you observe such events. That will make it easy to take notes on different students at once.

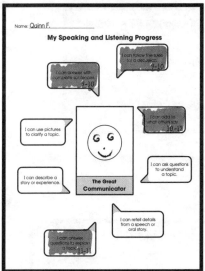

This sheet first serves as a teaching tool and then a self-assessment tool. Students will try to live up to their goals, so share the sheet before using it for self-assessment. Students will color the speech bubbles of skills they feel they have mastered. If desired, they may write the date inside each bubble. When they have colored every speech bubble, they may draw their own faces in the space above the caption "The Great Communicator." Consider rating students with this sheet twice a year.

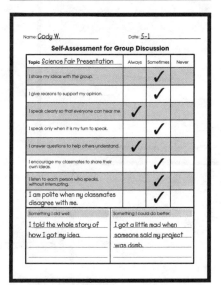

This form makes it easy for students to assess themselves on their participation in conversations and group discussions. The left column shows a list of desired speaking and listening attributes. Use the blank space to fill in another classroom rule or have the students do so. After signing and dating the form, students need only check off *Always*, *Sometimes*, or *Never*. After checking the appropriate boxes, have students write a sentence or two to tell something they did well and something they can do better next time.

Name: _____

Speaking and Listening Observations

Date _____
Event _____
_____

Participates in collaborative conversation

Speaks and listens in small and large groups

Follows rules for a discussion

Asks and answers questions about a topic

Uses complete sentences

Date _____
Event _____
_____

Participates in collaborative conversation

Speaks and listens in small and large groups

Follows rules for a discussion

Asks and answers questions about a topic

Uses complete sentences

Name: _____

My Speaking and Listening Progress

I can follow the rules for a discussion.

I can answer with complete sentences.

I can add to what others say.

I can use pictures to clarify a topic.

The Great Communicator

I can ask questions to understand a topic.

I can describe a story or experience.

I can retell details from a speech or oral story.

I can answer questions to explain a topic.

Name: _____ Date: _____

Self-Assessment for Group Discussion

Topic _____	Always	Sometimes	Never
I share my ideas with the group.			
I give reasons to support my opinion.			
I speak clearly so that everyone can hear me.			
I speak only when it is my turn to speak.			
I answer questions to help others understand.			
I encourage my classmates to share their own ideas.			
I listen to each person who speaks, without interrupting.			

Something I did well:	Something I could do better:
_____	_____
_____	_____
_____	_____
_____	_____

130

Language Standards Crosswalk

First Grade

Conventions of Standard English

- Use conventions of standard English grammar and usage in writing or speaking.
- Print all uppercase and lowercase letters.
- Use common, proper, and possessive nouns; singular and plural nouns with subject-verb agreement; personal, possessive, and indefinite pronouns; past, present, and future verbs; adjectives, conjunctions, and prepositions; and determiners such as *a, the, this,* and *that.*
- Write and expand complete simple and compound sentences.
- Use correct capitalization, punctuation, and spelling when writing.
- Capitalize dates and names of people; use commas and end punctuation.
- Use common spelling patterns and irregular words and phonetics to spell words.

Knowledge of Language (Begins in Grade 2)

Vocabulary Acquisition and Use

- Use sentence-level context clues to the meaning of words or phrases.
- Use frequently occurring affixes as a clue to the meaning of a word.
- Identify common root words and their inflectional forms.
- Understand word relationships and nuances in word meanings.
- Sort and define words by categories.
- Identify real-life connections between words and their use.
- Distinguish shades of meaning among verbs and adjectives.
- Use learned words and phrases, including common conjunctions such as *because.*

Third Grade

Conventions of Standard English

- Use conventions of standard English grammar and usage in writing or speaking.
- Understand and explain the functions of parts of speech, including regular and irregular plural nouns, abstract nouns, regular and irregular verbs, and verb tenses; ensure subject-verb and pronoun-antecedent agreement; use comparative and superlative adjectives and adverbs; and use coordinating and subordinating conjunctions.
- Produce simple, compound, and complex sentences.
- Use capitalization, punctuation, and spelling correctly when writing.
- Capitalize words in titles; use commas and quotation marks in dialogue; and form and use possessives.
- Use conventional spelling and spelling patterns to write words and to add suffixes.
- Consult reference materials to check and correct spellings.

Knowledge of Language

- Choose words and phrases for effect.
- Recognize differences between spoken and written standard English.

Vocabulary Acquisition and Use

- Flexibly use various strategies to understand unknown words on a third-grade level.
- Use context, affixes and roots as clues to the meaning of words or phrases; use glossaries or beginning dictionaries to clarify meaning.
- Understand figurative language, word relationships, and nuances in words.
- Distinguish the literal and nonliteral meanings of words and phrases in context.
- Identify real-life connections between words and their uses.
- Distinguish meaning among words that describe states of mind or certainty.
- Learn and use conversational, academic, and subject-specific vocabulary, including words that show time and place.

Language Concepts Checklist

Concept		Date(s) Taught				

Parts of Speech

With this sheet, it is easy to track the parts of speech you teach over time or in a unit. Record student names in the left-hand column. Nine parts of speech are listed. In the blank spaces below, mark the date you taught the concept in the left half of the blank. If you taught the concept to the whole group, it is only necessary to mark the date on the first line. In the right half of the blank, use a marking system such as a simple check mark or a 1-to-4 scale to indicate mastery.

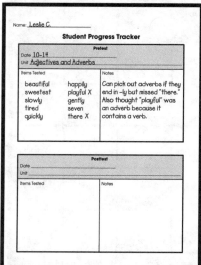

This form will help you track what material has been presented to individual students and if they mastered the material. Write the part(s) of speech presented. On the left side, list the items used to test the student. You may circle those that the students got correct or place marks next to any errors. On the right side, use the note section to record any observations or recommendations. The sheet holds two identical forms for use in pretesting and posttesting.

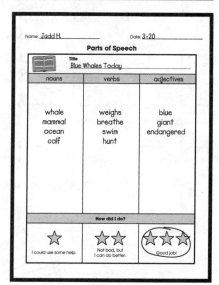

Use this versatile form to test a student's understanding of any of the parts of speech. Write the parts of speech you are studying above the three columns. Give the student a short text to read; either one of you can record the name of it in the title space. During or after the reading, the student should write any examples of the parts of speech listed in the correct spaces. Finally, the student should rate himself by circling one to three stars. If you also want to rate the student, use a different color of marker to circle your rating.

Parts of Speech

√ = Mastery / Students	Nouns	Collective Nouns	Irregular Nouns	Pronouns	Reflexive Pronouns	Verbs	Irregular Verbs	Adjectives	Adverbs

Name: _____

Student Progress Tracker

Pretest
Date _____
Unit _____

Items Tested	Notes

Posttest
Date _____
Unit _____

Items Tested	Notes

Parts of Speech

Title

_____

How did I do?		

I could use some help.

Not bad, but
I can do better.

Good job!

Sentence Construction

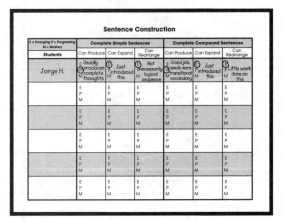

This is an ideal form to use when teaching simple and compound sentences. Record student names in the left-hand column. Students need to learn how to produce, expand, and rearrange simple and compound sentences. Use this sheet to track who has mastered these skills and who needs remediation. Circle *E*, *P*, or *M* to indicate skill level. This form offers a quick look at the group as a whole. Write dates or notes beside the rating scale as needed.

This form is a perfect tool for teaching students how to organize their thoughts into complete sentences. Ask students to imagine a scenario, real or make-believe, and then write answers to the five W's. From there, it is a hop and skip to writing complete sentences. After giving students feedback on the successes or challenges of the first one, have students try it again. Finally, ask students to rate themselves by coloring or circling the appropriate face.

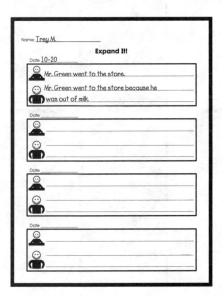

Students' first sentences are often short and without detail. Once students are more confident about writing complete sentences, they can move on to writing expanded sentences. To complete this form, write a simple sentence on the first line beside the teacher icon. If working with a group, write the sentence on the board and have students copy it. Ask students to think of a logical next part in the simple sentence. Tell them about linking words such as *and* and *because*. Students can then link their two thoughts into an expanded or compound sentence.

Sentence Construction

E = Emerging P = Progressing
M = Mastery

Students	Complete Simple Sentences			Complete Compound Sentences		
	Can Produce	Can Expand	Can Rearrange	Can Produce	Can Expand	Can Rearrange
	E P M	E P M	E P M	E P M	E P M	E P M
	E P M	E P M	E P M	E P M	E P M	E P M
	E P M	E P M	E P M	E P M	E P M	E P M
	E P M	E P M	E P M	E P M	E P M	E P M
	E P M	E P M	E P M	E P M	E P M	E P M
	E P M	E P M	E P M	E P M	E P M	E P M

Complete Sentences

Who _____   _____

Did What? _____   _____

When? _____   _____

Where? _____   _____

Why? _____   _____

Who _____   _____

Did What? _____   _____

When? _____   _____

Where? _____   _____

Why? _____   _____

I can write complete sentences.   ☺ 😐 ☹

Expand It!

Date _____

Date _____

Date _____

Date _____

Capitalization

With this sheet, it is easy to keep track of the rules of capitalization you teach over time or in a unit. Record student names in the left-hand column. Six capitalization rules are listed. In the blank divided spaces below, mark the date you taught each rule or place a check mark in the left half of the blank. If you taught the rule to the whole group, it is only necessary to mark the date on the first line. In the right half of the blank, use a marking system such as a simple check mark or a 1-to-4 scale to indicate mastery. Use the last column to take notes.

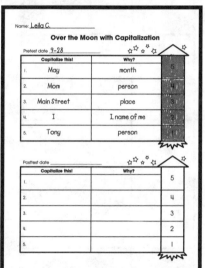

This fun sheet is set up for pretesting and posttesting. Students will use it to track their success at following capitalization rules. Students will look at sentences that contain capitalization errors. To add interest, write the sentences on index cards and set them up like a game of Scoot. When students have completed the sheet and you have checked their work, allow them to color the rocket appropriately. Have students add a happy face to the rocket if they achieve liftoff!

This sheet allows you to track the capitalization skills of a single student four times a year or four students separately. Give students a paragraph with capitalization errors. Students will write the name of the piece on the title line. As they read, they should look for capitalization errors. They can write any incorrect words on the left and the corrected words on the right. When finished, they should count the errors and write the number in the magnifying glass. Time-Saving Tip: Print this page on large adhesive labels to easily attach to the back of student samples. Visit our website for the template.

Conventions of Standard English Capitalization

Covered ☑ / Mastered ✓ Students	Beginning of a sentence	The word I	Names of people and places	Names of days, months, and holidays	Titles of books, games, and TV programs	Greetings and closings of letters	Notes

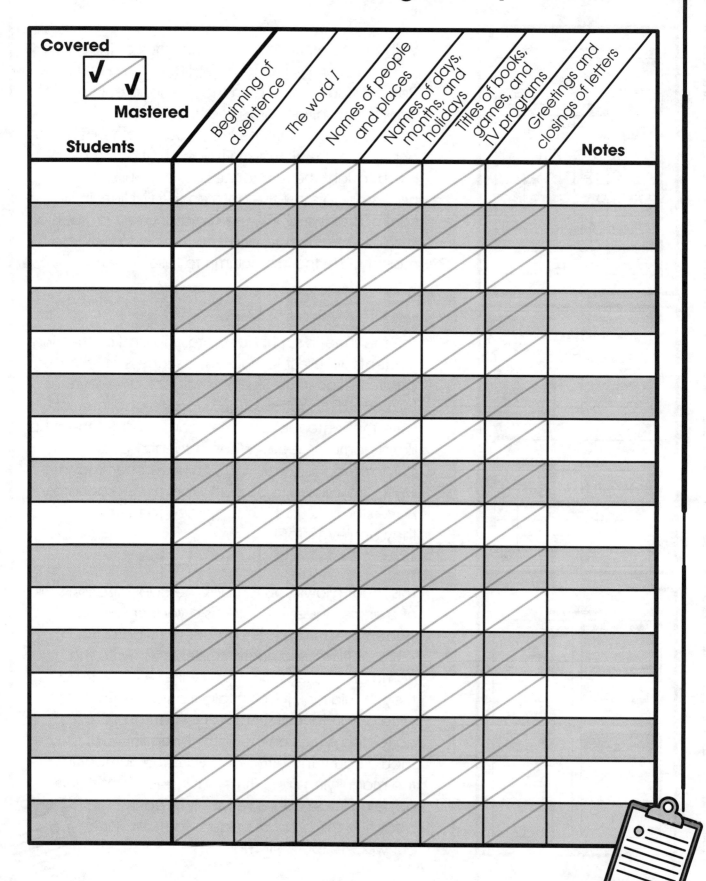

Name: _____

Over the Moon with Capitalization

Pretest date _____

Capitalize this!	Why?	
1.		5
2.		4
3.		3
4.		2
5.		1

Posttest date _____

Capitalize this!	Why?	
1.		5
2.		4
3.		3
4.		2
5.		1

Capitalization Detective

Name _____
Date _____
Title _____

I found ◯ **mistakes.**

_____ _____

_____ _____

_____ _____

_____ _____

_____ _____

Name _____
Date _____
Title _____

I found ◯ **mistakes.**

_____ _____

_____ _____

_____ _____

_____ _____

_____ _____

Name _____
Date _____
Title _____

I found ◯ **mistakes.**

_____ _____

_____ _____

_____ _____

_____ _____

_____ _____

Name _____
Date _____
Title _____

I found ◯ **mistakes.**

_____ _____

_____ _____

_____ _____

_____ _____

_____ _____

Punctuation

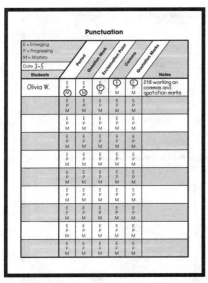

This class list will show at a glance which students have mastered which punctuation marks. Students should be able to recognize them, name them, and use them in appropriate places for mastery. Record student names in the left column. Five punctuation marks are listed in the next columns. Circle the level of mastery below each one. Color code your circles if you want to record levels at different times; show the coding in the space above *Notes*. Use the *Notes* section to record any observations.

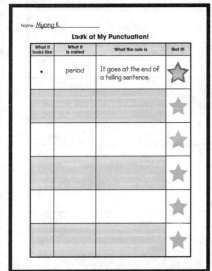

Use this simple form to allow students to show what they know about punctuation. In the left-hand column, they will draw the punctuation you request or just make a list of the ones they know. In the second column, students will write the name of the punctuation mark. In the third column, students will tell what the rule is. In the last column, students get a chance to congratulate themselves by tracing or coloring the star.

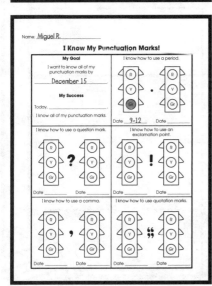

Students will use this form to show that they know how to use punctuation marks. This form has room for two assessments, so you may use it for pretesting and posttesting. Students can also complete it after they have mastered any one punctuation mark and dated the form accordingly. Have students set a date for mastering all five punctuation marks in the *My Goal* section. In each box, they can color, date, and rate their levels of mastery (green = mastered, yellow = progressing, and red = emerging). At the end of the unit, or when all marks are mastered, students can fill in the date in the *My Success* block.

Punctuation

Students	Period	Question Mark	Exclamation Point	Comma	Quotation Marks	Notes
	E P M	E P M	E P M	E P M	E P M	
	E P M	E P M	E P M	E P M	E P M	
	E P M	E P M	E P M	E P M	E P M	
	E P M	E P M	E P M	E P M	E P M	
	E P M	E P M	E P M	E P M	E P M	
	E P M	E P M	E P M	E P M	E P M	
	E P M	E P M	E P M	E P M	E P M	
	E P M	E P M	E P M	E P M	E P M	
	E P M	E P M	E P M	E P M	E P M	
	E P M	E P M	E P M	E P M	E P M	

E = Emerging
P = Progressing
M = Mastery

Date

Name: _____

L★★k at My Punctuation!

What it looks like	What it is called	What the rule is	Got it!
			★
			★
			★
			★
			★
			★

Name: _____

I Know My Punctuation Marks!

My Goal	I know how to use a period.

My Goal

I want to know all of my punctuation marks by

_____.

My Success

Today, _____,

I know all of my punctuation marks.

I know how to use a period.

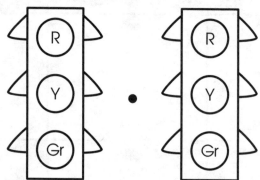

Date _____   Date _____

I know how to use a question mark.

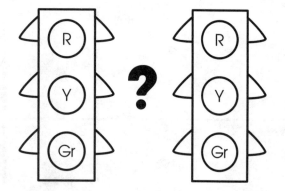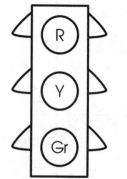

Date _____   Date _____

I know how to use an exclamation point.

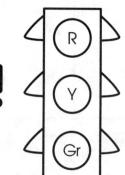

Date _____   Date _____

I know how to use a comma.

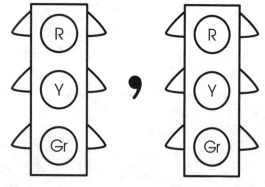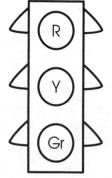

Date _____   Date _____

I know how to use quotation marks.

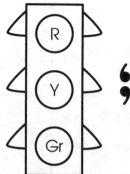

Date _____   Date _____

Contractions and Possessives

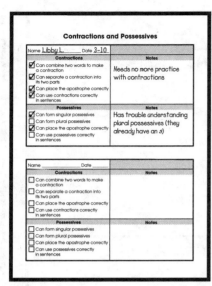

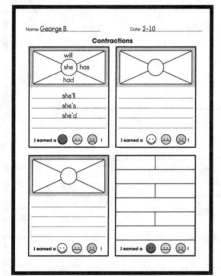

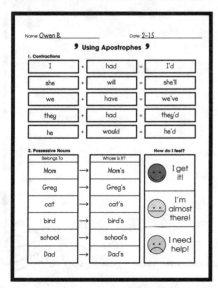

Second graders need to be able to combine, separate, place, and use contractions, as well as be able to form, place, and use possessives. This sheet makes it simple to track which students understand contractions and possessives. Record each student's name and date in the top left strip. Below, check off the skills the student has mastered; leave the boxes blank if you have not yet taught the skills or if the student has not mastered them. Use the *Notes* section to record any observations.

This sheet gives students four opportunities to practice putting together and taking apart contractions. In the first three boxes, write or have students write a pronoun in the circle. In the surrounding blanks, write verbs that can be joined with that pronoun to make a contraction. The students will join the pronoun with each verb to make contractions. In the last section, write or have students write a contraction in the long box. Then, students can write the two words that make the contraction in the boxes above. Below each box is a place for students to rate themselves by coloring or circling the appropriate face.

Students can show what they know about using apostrophes with this sheet. Second graders need to be able to use the apostrophe with contractions and possessive nouns. Use this sheet after teaching either or both. You may duplicate it for use in pretesting and posttesting. After students have filled in each half, check their work and give feedback. Then, allow students to color or circle the appropriate face.

Contractions and Possessives

Name _____ Date _____

Contractions	Notes
☐ Can combine two words to make a contraction	
☐ Can separate a contraction into its two parts	
☐ Can place the apostrophe correctly	
☐ Can use contractions correctly in sentences	

Possessives	Notes
☐ Can form singular possessives	
☐ Can form plural possessives	
☐ Can place the apostrophe correctly	
☐ Can use possessives correctly in sentences	

Name _____ Date _____

Contractions	Notes
☐ Can combine two words to make a contraction	
☐ Can separate a contraction into its two parts	
☐ Can place the apostrophe correctly	
☐ Can use contractions correctly in sentences	

Possessives	Notes
☐ Can form singular possessives	
☐ Can form plural possessives	
☐ Can place the apostrophe correctly	
☐ Can use possessives correctly in sentences	

Contractions

I earned a 🙂 😐 🙁 !

I earned a 🙂 😐 🙁 !

I earned a 🙂 😐 🙁 !

I earned a 🙂 😐 🙁 !

 , Using Apostrophes ,

I. Contractions

☐	+	☐	=	☐
☐	+	☐	=	☐
☐	+	☐	=	☐
☐	+	☐	=	☐
☐	+	☐	=	☐

2. Possessive Nouns

How do I feel?

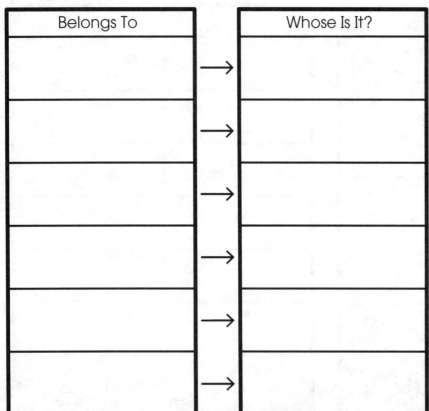

Belongs To		Whose Is It?
	→	
	→	
	→	
	→	
	→	
	→	

I get it!

I'm almost there!

I need help!

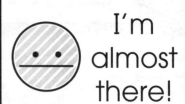

Vocabulary Acquisition

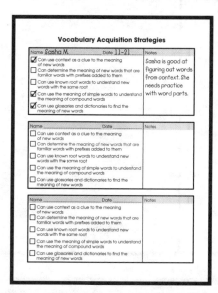

Use this form at any time to track students' progress as they grow as readers. You may also use it in conference with individual students or with whole groups. The form will give you a quick look at students' abilities to use various strategies to learn new words. Keep these forms at hand so that you can make notes any time you observe a student successfully using a particular strategy. Use the *Notes* section to record any observations.

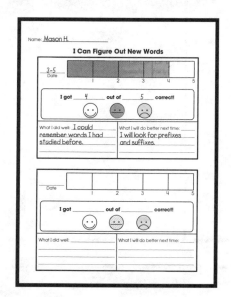

This is an opportunity for students to show what they know of recent, new vocabulary. Give students five new words in context or without, allowing them to use any of various strategies to figure out the words' meanings. After receiving feedback on their efforts, allow them to date the form and rate themselves by coloring the bar appropriately and shading the appropriate face to show how they feel about their work. In addition, have students tell what they did well and what they will do better next time.

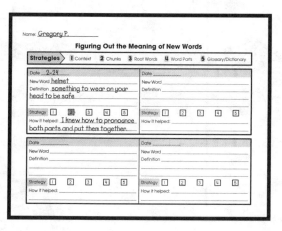

Students can decode new vocabulary if they know various strategies. This form lists five strategies, but add others that you teach. After introducing these strategies, give students a short list of unfamiliar words. Allow them to decode words using any of the listed strategies. Students will write a word and its definition. They can then color or shade the number of the strategy that helped them. Finally, they should write how the strategy helped them.

Vocabulary Acquisition Strategies

Name _____ Date _____	Notes
☐ Can use context as a clue to the meaning of new words ☐ Can determine the meaning of new words that are familiar words with prefixes added to them ☐ Can use known root words to understand new words with the same root ☐ Can use the meaning of simple words to understand the meaning of compound words ☐ Can use glossaries and dictionaries to find the meaning of new words	

Name _____ Date _____	Notes
☐ Can use context as a clue to the meaning of new words ☐ Can determine the meaning of new words that are familiar words with prefixes added to them ☐ Can use known root words to understand new words with the same root ☐ Can use the meaning of simple words to understand the meaning of compound words ☐ Can use glossaries and dictionaries to find the meaning of new words	

Name _____ Date _____	Notes
☐ Can use context as a clue to the meaning of new words ☐ Can determine the meaning of new words that are familiar words with prefixes added to them ☐ Can use known root words to understand new words with the same root ☐ Can use the meaning of simple words to understand the meaning of compound words ☐ Can use glossaries and dictionaries to find the meaning of new words	

Name: _____

I Can Figure Out New Words

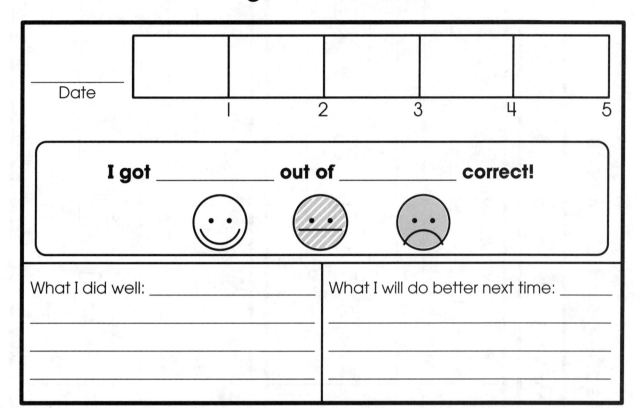

Date _____

1	2	3	4	5

I got _____ **out of** _____ **correct!**

What I did well: _____

_____

_____

_____

What I will do better next time: _____

_____

_____

_____

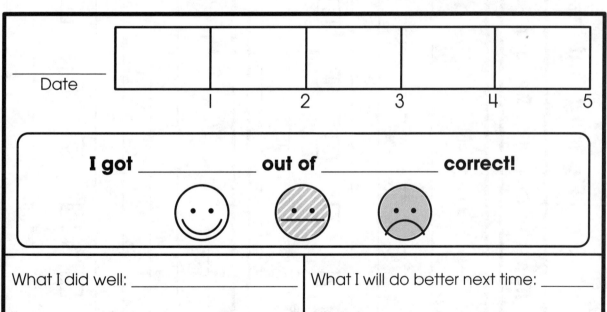

Date _____

1	2	3	4	5

I got _____ **out of** _____ **correct!**

What I did well: _____

_____

_____

_____

What I will do better next time: _____

_____

_____

_____

Name: _____

Figuring Out the Meaning of New Words

Strategies

1 Context **2** Chunks **3** Root Words **4** Word Parts **5** Glossary/Dictionary

---

Date _____

New Word _____

Definition _____
_____

Strategy [1] [2] [3] [4] [5]

How it helped: _____
_____

Date _____

New Word _____

Definition _____
_____

Strategy [1] [2] [3] [4] [5]

How it helped: _____
_____

Date _____

New Word _____

Definition _____
_____

Strategy [1] [2] [3] [4] [5]

How it helped: _____
_____

Date _____

New Word _____

Definition _____
_____

Strategy [1] [2] [3] [4] [5]

How it helped: _____
_____

Academic Vocabulary

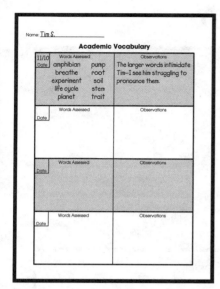

In recent years, there has been an instructional shift focusing on academic vocabulary. Students need to learn the vocabulary of the content areas in order to understand the content. As you pre-teach unit vocabulary, use this form to keep track of the words you have taught and assessed. Use the observations section to note learning behaviors and follow-up plans.

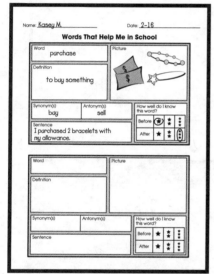

Use this form as students encounter unfamiliar words in the content areas. They should write a word in the top-left space and then skip to the bottom right space to rate how well they already know the word. They may use any strategy to figure out the word's meaning. Then, have them draw a picture to represent the word or remind themselves of its meaning. Next, they can write synonyms and antonyms for the word and use it in a sentence. Once they have completed the form, they should return to the bottom right and rate how well they understand the word now.

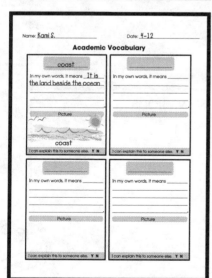

Use this simple form over and over again to allow students to work with new vocabulary. Use the form for any vocabulary lesson but particularly when teaching target words needed for mastering content. Students will fill in the top box with a single vocabulary word and then write its definition in their own words. Next, students can draw a picture to show their understanding or remind themselves of the word's meaning. The best test of mastery is being able to explain the word to someone. Have students rate themselves by circling *Y* for *yes* or *N* for *no*.

Name: _____

Academic Vocabulary

Date	Words Assessed	Observations
Date	Words Assessed	Observations
Date	Words Assessed	Observations
Date	Words Assessed	Observations

Words That Help Me in School

Word	Picture

Definition

Synonym(s)	Antonym(s)	How well do I know this word?

	Before	★	★★	★★★
	After	★	★★	★★★

Sentence

Word	Picture

Definition

Synonym(s)	Antonym(s)	How well do I know this word?

	Before	★	★★	★★★
	After	★	★★	★★★

Sentence

Academic Vocabulary

_____

In my own words, it means _____

_____

_____

_____

_____ .

Picture

I can explain this to someone else. **Y N**

_____

In my own words, it means _____

_____

_____

_____

_____ .

Picture

I can explain this to someone else. **Y N**

_____

In my own words, it means _____

_____

_____

_____

_____ .

Picture

I can explain this to someone else. **Y N**

_____

In my own words, it means _____

_____

_____

_____

_____ .

Picture

I can explain this to someone else. **Y N**
